Danny Gilchrist stumbled into a career as a large animal veterinarian when, by happenstance, he tagged along to the birth of a lamb, an act he attributes to divine intervention. He has collected memories of his life and work in *Fella,* named for beloved childhood pet. It's a thoroughly engrossing work.

Gilchrist spent a lifetime driving the back roads of upstate New York, tending to dairy cows, sheep, and just as often the farmers who relied on them for a livelihood. A typical day might find him awakened by an emergency call at 2 a.m. A devout Mormon, he views his work as part of his larger mission. The juxtaposition of clean living with a job that frequently leaves one covered in manure is the subject of numerous jokes.

When Gilchrist describes his job, the stories are addictive: You feel as if you're there in the barn, often in life-or-death circumstances; the triumphs and tragedies hit home boldly. *Fella* is hard to put down. When Gilchrist amputates the leg of an injured chinchilla and reassures the owner that the animal will be fine, his heart shines through. He reminds readers of the trust animals place in us to be their friends and guardians, and sets an example few of us could equal.

—BlueInk Review

FELLA

Dear Gary,

Thank you for your hospitality. You are exactly who I envisioned. Thank you for your service to our own species & to the animal kingdom. I hope you enjoy these true stories from my life. Your brother

Dan. G.

FELLA

Danny K. Gilchrist

To order additional copies of this book, contact:
Xlibris LLC
1-888-795-4274
www.Xlibris.com
Orders@Xlibris.com
552378

Contents

Preface 9

Introduction 11

Chapter One   Bloat 13

Chapter Two   College Days 22

Chapter Three   Christmas 36

Chapter Four   Arizona! 42

Chapter Five   Bishop Gilchrist 55

Chapter Six   Poochie 72

Chapter Seven   Quiet Heroes 79

Chapter Eight   On the Road and Present Day 86

Chapter Nine   Home is Where the Heart is 112

Chapter Ten   Winter Sabbath 119

PREFACE

Last year, I commissioned a painting in oil of myself holding a newborn calf. I gave the painting to my children as a Christmas gift. It represents their childhood. When I'm dead and gone, they will think when they look at it of the countless hours, days, months, and years they spent riding around the back roads of New York from predawn until sometimes late into the night, doctoring animals of all sizes and temperaments. They would awaken early in the morning on their own, dress, and don their rubber boots so I would not leave without them. By the time they started kindergarten, they witnessed birth, death, disease, injury, and triumph over sickness, defeat, and helplessness. So many life lessons taught to them and to me, if we would just open our eyes and hearts to what was evident before us. Someone mockingly told me I was preaching from a trough in relating the experiences and lessons learned in my life with animals. There is none so blind as he who will not see. Thank you to my children and my wife, Judy, for your interest and understanding in what is to me a sacred calling, and thank you, Lord, for that call to serve.

Introduction

The title of the book is in honor of our family dog when I was five years old. He, above all others, was and is responsible for my love of animals. His story is told in this journal.

Being a large-animal veterinarian in upstate New York allows one a lot of time for thought out there on the highway. For many years, my truck was my home for twelve to eighteen hours out of the day. In my last year on the road, I listened to sixty-five unabridged books on tape as I traveled between farms. I got to know myself better than most people did, as I considered issues of the day and formulated opinions on this subject or that and defended those positions in open debate with myself as I traversed the hills and valleys of Otsego, Madison, Herkimer, Oneida, and Chenango counties. Many days I would travel over three hundred miles by day's end in the course of my duties. I had neither the time nor the desire to record my adventures except in the occasional talk I was asked to give at church, and then I would try to relate a story that would hold the attention of my audience and relate it to a gospel purpose or lesson. In the doing, I began to realize that many of my adventures carried with them a valuable life lesson that I had just taken for granted. I was blessed with work, and throughout my career, I have been very busy taking care of the creatures I love.

As I approach the end of my career, I find as I slow down that I have the time and the inclination to review past years and adventures and see in them profound and touching lessons that have shaped my life and knocked some edges off and made me much more sensitive and compassionate for all species including my own for the predicaments we all get into and then have to ask for help. If I had one wish at this point in my life, it would be that I could be a healer of body and spirit. As a doctor of veterinary medicine, I can only assist Mother Nature and the healing processes of living organisms toward repair. My wish would be that I could just touch living beings of all species and make them whole. And at the same time, that I could mend a broken heart. I content myself with being a helper.

This book is a collection of true stories that have happened in my life and career that my Maker has preserved in the memory cells of my mind for which I am forever grateful. They have come back to me in living color. My children grew up on the road with me and traveled with me when they weren't in school. We enjoyed a relationship that most didn't realize, as we worked together day and night, and they came to realize that whatever the problem we were faced with when we entered a barn, we weren't leaving until the problem was solved, so they are witnesses that these stories are true. Some of the entries are thoughts and emotions that have come to me in much the same way that they would as I drove in solitude around the countryside, tending to the medical needs of my four-legged friends who happened to have owners.

CHAPTER ONE

Bloat

I was called to a farm at suppertime one night many years ago for a cow that was bloating. Left unchecked, she would suffocate when her stomach expanded so much that her diaphragm couldn't move to invite air into her lungs. A cow's stomach is a huge fermentation vat constantly producing gas, which is exhausted up the esophagus in the form of giant methane burps. If the esophagus is obstructed, the gas accumulates. Such was the case. When I arrived, I found that the cows were being fed cull potatoes because the farmer was so poor he couldn't buy feed. His neighbor who grew potatoes let him have his culls to give to the cows. They were sorry-looking cows and producing very little milk, so the farmer was on a downhill slide, soon to go out of business. The cow in question had a potato stuck in her esophagus and was also on a rapid downhill slide.

I held her head up and stuck my hand between razor-sharp molars to the back of her mouth and beyond, so my arm was down her throat, almost up to my shoulder. I grasped the potato, but I couldn't get a good grip on it. Then all of a sudden, the cow regurgitated my arm and the potato. There was a loud crunch as she bit the potato with her molars then swallowed it. Then all that gas accumulating in her rumen exploded in my face, but it was nevertheless a lovely thing. The anxious farmer standing next to me cried out with glee, "You did it, Doc! By the Jesus, you did it." And by the Jesus, I had. She was all better in an instant. We went to the house so he could write a check to give me. I stepped into the kitchen, where all his children were seated at the table for supper. They were ages eight to twelve. All of them were bald. I realized they must be suffering from malnutrition. Supper was being cooked: potato pancakes.

If they were good enough to keep the cows alive, I guess they were good enough for his family. He gave me a check and thanked me profusely for coming. I went out to my truck, got in, and started up my old friend and cranked up the heater. I just sat there for a few minutes with a lump in my throat. It wasn't a potato. Then I got out of my truck and went to the barn. I handed my farmer back his check and said, "There's no charge for tonight." I drove home very slowly, taking in all the beautiful trees and meadows and cows grazing that I passed by so quickly on other days, barely even noticing them. When I arrived home, I stood outside our house and observed every nook and cranny of it. I saw the kids' bikes lying on the grass and shed a tear. I went slowly up the stairs and into the house and hugged Judy and each of the children. I was grateful for every blessing we had and every crust of bread. It's not an easy life I have lived, but as I traveled out into the lonely night, I have never felt alone. So many lessons learned in the solitude of my work.

They that be with us are more than they that be with them. 2 Kings 6:16.

As a little boy of four, I lived at a time when Canada was coming into the twentieth century. We had a milkman who delivered dairy products daily with a horse-drawn milk vehicle. The milk was cooled by big blocks of ice that were cut out of the river in winter and stored in ice houses so that the ice would stay frozen and be available through the summer. As children, we would have the milkman chip off a slab of ice with his ice pick and wrap tissue around it and lick it like an icicle. Our household refrigerator was cooled with ice, and my mother cooked our meals on a cast-iron woodstove. The bathroom was out in the backyard, and our baths were taken weekly in a steel washtub in the kitchen. Yes, I am *that* old! We had an English bulldog that was my constant companion. Our family never gave him a name; we just called him Fella as a puppy, and that became his name. As a boy of four and five, he was my daily companion and best friend. At noontime every day, I would listen to a radio program for children (there was no television). My mother made me a butter-and-sugar sandwich with homemade bread, Fella lay sprawled out on his side on the kitchen floor, and I lay at right angles to him, using his abdomen as a pillow. That was peace and contentment.

He would cover my whole face with his broad tongue. He loved me so, and I him. I believe he was the inspiration behind my career choice. Fella died when I was only five years old, some fifty-six years ago, but I remember him vividly still as though it were only yesterday. His picture stands on my desk in my office at home. It is a great comfort to me to know that animals are without sin, that they have a spirit, and that they are eternal in nature. In a sense, they are celestial beings in their earthly sojourn. Their innocence has softened my soul and taught me many lessons—on coping with life, unconditional love, simple faith, and acceptance of the course of events that shape our lives. In almost every way, our young children are similar to my animal friends. It is a great responsibility that we as parents and teachers carry, caring for and teaching the little ones.

I often reflect on the events that led to my decision to seek a career in veterinary medicine. I grew up in the city, and the only exposure I had to veterinary medicine was the few animals that we had as pets, Fella being the most memorable. We did not have a lot of money, so our visits to the veterinarian were few and far between. At the age of nineteen, I was called to serve a two-year mission for our church. My call was to France and Switzerland. I spent two months studying language and religion at the language training mission before leaving for Geneva for twenty-two months. I was an enthusiastic missionary for the first few months, but discouragement set in after a year of getting doors closed in my face and lack of response to the message I brought. I didn't really blame people. They were in a comfortable pew; why change? Nevertheless, I believed in our message and its importance to people's lives, so I continued. It was 1970, and the Vietnam War was raging. I was a Canadian missionary, but most of my companions were Americans, so the impending draft awaiting their return from their missions weighed heavily on their minds. At that time, I was serving in Geneva. My impression, right or wrong, was that the French-speaking Swiss tended to look down upon the natives of France.

One afternoon, I knocked on an apartment door in Geneva. A gentleman answered the door, and I told him who we were and asked if we could have a few minutes to talk with him. He became very irate and said in a loud voice in beautiful French with a musical Swiss accent, "Why don't you Americans get out of Vietnam before you come over here preaching to us?" To which I replied, "Je ne suis pas Americain, je suis Canadien." (I am not American; I am Canadian.) To which he replied, getting angrier, "Canadien, Americain, c'est tout la meme chose." (Canadian, American, it's all the same thing.) I calmly responded, "Monsieur, vous est Francais?" (Sir, you are French?) He straightened his back and said with great pride and somewhat pompously, "Non . . . je suis Suisse!" (No . . . I am Swiss.) To which I observed, "Suisse, Francais, c'est tout la meme chose!" (Swiss, French, it's all the same thing.) He ended the conversation by punching me in the chest. I pushed him away toward his door, and I saw his wife's hand on his shoulder pulling him back into the apartment and slamming the door in our faces. I thought, *You know, I didn't come over here for this. I mean only goodwill, but that's not the way it's working out.*

I called my parents and my mission president and informed them that I was going home, back to Canada. I had had enough. They listened sympathetically but asked me to give it a little more time. I had been out a year, and I had a year to go. It seemed like an eternity, but I understood their concern for me and how I would look back on this period with regret as I got older. I agreed to give it a little more time. I stayed another year, to the end of my mission. During that time, I had some high points, but I was counting the days to my release. I was twenty-one years old and had no clue what I wanted to do for a career. I had no special aptitude nor desire nor inclination toward any vocation. I started my mission with no real goals in life except to serve the Lord and dedicate two years fully to that end and then see what came next.

On about December 15, in the last week of my mission, my companion and I were having dinner with a young Swiss family at their home in Vevey.

After the meal, they asked to be excused so they could go down to the shed in their backyard to check on a ewe that was having a lamb. I had never witnessed such a thing and asked if I could tag along, to which they were happy to consent. I watched them wash up, then soap up, then put their hands inside the sheep to manipulate the lamb's head and feet, which were out of sight. I watched them deliver the lifeless lamb, laying it on its side, all wet and motionless, on the clear straw in the pen. They patiently rubbed him vigorously, and his mother started licking him with her rough tongue. Within a couple of minutes, there was some movement, then a bleat. Soon he was sitting up, trying to stand. Then after a few moments, he was standing on his own. By the time I left, he was nursing. I was amazed and exhilarated to see life come into that tiny lifeless being. To this city boy who had never seen such a thing, it was the biggest miracle I had witnessed during my two-year mission. I forgot about the experience and left for Canada the following week and back to my life.

I worked for a few months, saving money for college. I had no idea what I wanted to do with my life. I had fulfilled my lifelong goal of serving the Lord for two years, but beyond that, my life was an empty slate with no particular future in mind. I quit work and packed a duffel bag, put out my thumb, and headed for California to visit my sister in San Jose and my brother in Anaheim. I returned five weeks later and went back to work. During that time away, I contemplated what I might choose for a career. As I thought about it more earnestly, I remembered the lambing I had witnessed so many months before. Suddenly, it was like a light illuminated my heart and the darkness in my mind as I realized that I had been shown my life's work in that little shed in that tiny village in far-off Switzerland by a being to whom I had dedicated two years of my life. From that moment on, I focused on veterinary medicine, entering college, studying through the night, gaining experience with animals, and doing everything I could to ensure admittance to the Ontario Veterinary College. There were 120 openings and over 1,200 applicants each year, and I was told of the unlikelihood of being accepted, but I kept my mind on the job at hand and focused on the future. I shall always remember that Christmas and be forever grateful for that defining moment in my life that came in the closing hours of my mission and that I stayed to finish what I started.

Life is not easy. As I sit at my desk contemplating my woes, our black cat jumps into the middle of my paperwork and is purring up a storm. He lies on his side with his paws outstretched, wanting to play. He doesn't know my troubles or worries; he just knows he loves me. He came to our clinic as a tiny kitten with a huge infected eye. I told the owner we would need to remove it. He agreed and left him with us. I did the surgery the next morning. Two weeks went by, and his owner never returned. So this homeless, unwanted one-eyed kitten became ours.

We took him home and changed his name to Johnny One Eye. He carries on with one eye like nothing happened. I rejoice that he has found happiness out of what was a desperate situation. I love animals. They wake up one morning homeless and missing one eye and just carry on like nothing happened. They harbor ill will toward no one. I want to be just like that when I grow up.

Last Christmas Eve, we were trying to wrap appointments up at the clinic at noon so everyone could be home with their families. A young woman came in at noon with an eight-week-old puppy she had just purchased. The woman came with an interpreter as she didn't understand English. The puppy was very sick, with vomiting and diarrhea. It had dreaded parvovirus, which is highly contagious to other animals and carries a high mortality rate in young puppies. The owner was financially destitute but loved this little puppy she had acquired a few hours earlier. I told her that to treat this condition would cost several hundred dollars, and the prognosis, even with IV treatments and constant care, was poor for such a young puppy. I advised her to return to the breeder and ask her to take care of treatment of the puppy until it was better, since she had just come from there, and the breeder would need to take responsibility for the cost of treatment. She agreed and left in tears.

Just as I was leaving the clinic to go home, the phone rang. It was a client who had an older dog that was scratching himself raw from a skin allergy.

She said she was broke until payday and wondered if there was anything she could do for the dog before she had the money to come in to have him treated. She was very subdued and worried about her dog. I told her she could give the dog a bath every other day and Benadryl to relieve the itching but that we should see him as soon as she could get the money together. Then I went home to prepare for Christmas and forgot about the clinic and my patients for a few hours. We spent the afternoon very busily making last-minute preparations for the exciting day ahead. I went to bed at 1:00 AM, having put the last of the presents under the tree for Christmas morning. I was exhausted and instantly fell into a deep sleep when my head hit the pillow. Two hours later, at 3:00 AM, I sat straight up in bed, wide-awake. I was thinking of those last two people I talked to at the clinic. I said to myself, *You just told two people there was no room at the inn.* I was in a cold sweat at the thought of my lack of compassion. I jumped out of bed and thought through the events of the end of hours. I remembered that I had their phone numbers written on pieces of paper on my desk at the clinic, but I had thrown them in the garbage after speaking with them. Maybe the garbage hadn't been taken out.

As I dressed, I said a prayer telling the Lord that that man at the clinic wasn't the man my mother had raised but a man that was tired and trying to go home for Christmas. I asked Him to please give me another chance to be my mother's son. I put on my winter coat and drove up the road to the clinic. I found the number to the young woman with the sick puppy, but the other number had gone out to the Dumpster with the garbage. I am not one to give up easily, so I got a flashlight and went out to the Dumpster. I had to get a ladder and reach over the top, down into the middle of it, and I picked out the top bag, hoping it was the one with the note. I took it inside where the light was better and it was warm. I emptied the contents on the floor of our treatment room and started to go through the contents. Friend, you don't ever want to have to go through a garbage bag from a veterinary clinic. I thought to myself, *What are you doing? Why are you going through this garbage at three on Christmas morning?* Then I thought, *No, this is altogether fitting that you are doing this. It is a just punishment for your indifference.*

Then joy as I found the missing phone number. I replaced everything in the bag and returned it to the Dumpster. Then I waited patiently for the seconds, minutes, and hours to pass before 7:00 AM came and I could call these people. I prayed that the young woman would still have the puppy and that both clients would be willing to come to the clinic on Christmas morning so I could care for their beloved pets. I made the calls, and both were willing to come in! At 9:00 AM, the puppy arrived, and I gave it some fluids and medications while they waited. He had improved considerably, so I felt better sending him home with treatments they could do at home and the promise that they would call tomorrow to report his condition. As I completed the visit, I put some folded money in their hands and told them there was no charge for today's visit and I wanted them to buy some things for the puppy with the money I gave them. They left for home relieved that their friend had been tended to.

The second lady arrived with her teenage son and their aging dog. Sure enough, he had a large bloody, raw spot that he had been chewing on incessantly. I gave him some injections to stop the itching and medications to follow up with at home. I told the mother that there was no charge for today and held out some money for her as a Christmas gift. She said, "No, you've done enough, thank you." I nodded but put the money in her son's pocket and said, "Buy your mother something nice for Christmas." We all shed a few tears, hugged, and parted to our homes and families for Christmas. As I left the clinic, I said a prayer and thanked the Lord for this opportunity He gave me to turn back the hands of time just this once and be the man my mother raised. It occurred to me that the Christmas season we celebrate had profound meaning to me this year as I was forgiven of my trespass and given a new start.

The duties of a large-animal veterinarian are many and varied. One minute we might be delivering a tiny lamb from a small ewe having lambing problems, and the next minute we might be operating on a 1,700-pound cow with a twisted stomach.

Some of the duties are pleasant, some are joyful, and some are filthy, leaving us obliged to return to base, shower up, and continue. Some duties are a nightmare. I have been called out on a few occasions to barn fires; these visits are terrible. I was called at midnight to a farm near Gilbertsville a few years ago. The dairy was on fire. The cows were show cows, their genetics known across the nation by dairymen. Each animal had a name and a history, and great expectations were invested in each calf and yearling. Most of the cows had been chased out of the barn, but the future of the farm— the yearlings and calves—had not fared so well. The main barn was still on fire, and the firemen were fighting the flames to keep them out of the smoke-filled heifer wing, where I had to perform my sad duty of ending the pain and misery of the animals caught in the heat and smoke. I worked there for three hours as the firemen worked ahead of me, doing their duty.

Finally, the flames were doused, the animals that could be treated were medicated, and the rest of my duties were completed. I left for home shocked, defeated, drained, exhausted, and numb to what I had witnessed and experienced. I was so tired on arrival at home that I collapsed on the couch in our living room, coveralls and all. I awoke the next morning, and our whole house reeked of barn fire. My clothes and I carried that horrible odor into our home. My wife and family said little, but the children didn't waste any time heading out the door for school. It is impossible to leave such a place unaffected.

Similarly, we can't help but be influenced to some degree by the people and things we choose to associate with, whether for good or evil. We carry with us the sum of our experiences. Many of those experiences can't be helped. We are obligated by the terms of our employment or the circumstances of our lives to be exposed to them. But many of our experiences come as a result of our own choices. 'I am the master of my fate, the captain of my soul.' (Invictus' by William Ernest Henley)

CHAPTER TWO

College Days

In December of 1973, I received word from the Ontario Veterinary College that I was accepted into the doctor of veterinary medicine program and would be in the OVC '78 class. Judy and I were married on December 15, 1973. That acceptance was about the only wedding gift I had for her, but it was to me the most wonderful present for both of us. It defined our future together. It also opened the door to many hills and valleys, to many great and joyous moments, and to many times of deep despair. At the time, I had little experience in working with farm animals. I decided that if I were going to be treating and operating on large animals, I better get some experience working with them, understanding their husbandry, and having an appreciation of their owner's daily routine, challenges, outlook, and philosophy so I would be more able to assess the likelihood of my diagnoses and treatment plans being accepted and followed.

I went to the guidance office at the college and found a list of farmers in the area who had advertised there in the past for student summer work. The second phone call was to an elderly lady who owned a small family farm not too far from the college. I explained that I was looking for summer work. She asked if I had any experience, to which I replied none. She politely and sympathetically replied that she really couldn't afford to hire me if that was the case. I told her how much I would need, and she hired me on the spot, saying that for that amount, they could afford to train me.

So began a lifelong friendship and a four-year summer and weekend during the school year, working relationship. I learned so much working on the farm that directly related to my future employment as a veterinarian. I learned the day-to-day routine of farmers, the financial challenges, and the worry whether crops would be sufficient in quantity and nutritional value to sustain through the winter and of excellent-enough quality to allow the cows to produce milk in quantities that would allow a profit. I learned how to clean calf pens, bed the cow stalls, build and fix fences, combine grain, harvest hay, run tractors, spread manure, prepare fields for planting, sow crops, and fertilize. I learned to be concerned for each cow and watch them twice daily for any sign of illness: not eating, depressed milk production, and so forth. I learned of the ever-present challenges to farm profitability, and I learned of compassion for the animals, who were the mechanism by which the farm continued.

During this time of our lives, we needed to have a car, but with the budget we lived with, the cars were ones we nursed along day to day and came with a long list of potential problems. One car we had was sporty and a nice-looking machine that I purchased for $500. It would run perfectly for a time, but at the most inopportune moments, it would just die. Somehow I figured out that if I crawled underneath the back end and disconnected the fuel line to the gas tank and then blew on the line until I heard air bubbling into the gas tank, then rejoined the fuel line to the tank, it would run fine for a few days then conk out again. I supposed that there must be some rust in the tank that was loosening up and clogging the line, just like a bladder stone. I usually would end up with a face full of gas before I could rejoin the line.

One Sunday morning, we were on our way to church with our two small children, ages six months and two years. We were in the country, halfway there, when the car decided it was time for me to crawl under in my good clothes and give a good blow. I was rewarded with the same face full of gasoline and a car that would fire up and roll again. We arrived at church on time but with me reeking of gasoline. I was grateful that neither Judy nor I were smokers nor anyone in the congregation, because if anyone had lit up around me, we would have gone up in flames.

We lived at that time in a small town about fifteen miles from the university. It was about halfway between the farm and the college. When I left in the morning, I would be gone for the whole day, at classes or studying in the library. I didn't want to leave Judy and the children without a car all that time, so I found a bus service that went every hour and a half back and forth between the two towns. One late afternoon lecture in biostatistics found me waiting afterward for the bus. It was 5:00 PM, and I was tired and hungry and cold. It was snowing and blowing outside, so I waited in the lobby of the lecture hall, watching the road for the bus. Biostatistics was a mystery to me when I first started the course. It took me a while to realize that I shouldn't try to understand how the probability formulae worked but concentrate on how to use them to define probability that certain things might or might not occur. This is important in deciding whether risk is worth result in treatment. After I had that epiphany, I excelled at the subject and was able to ask and answer questions during lecture. It was a good feeling of accomplishment that I had mastered at least this part of my studies.

Just as I spotted my bus approaching in the distance, a young man with a strong foreign accent approached me. "Excuse me, sir, but you seem to have a good understanding of this course, could you explain a few things to me that I'm having trouble with?" I had to listen carefully to understand his broken English. I looked at him anxiously as I spotted the bus closing in on my stop. I would have to hurry to catch it or wait another hour and a half for the last run of the day. Supper, Judy, and James and Erin, our children, were waiting for me. I started to say that I would have to explain it another time because my bus was here. Just as I opened my mouth to speak, this came to mind: "Inasmuch as ye have done it unto one of the least of these my brethren, ye have done it unto me." (Matthew 25:40) I closed the door and stayed to help my brother.

Monday found me back in class at the college. Pathology is an interesting subject, putting another piece in the puzzle of illness and disease. Most pathology professors like to take slides of autopsies for future reference and teaching. Almost every lecture has about twenty minutes devoted to viewing slides projected onto a large screen at the front of the lecture hall. The professor will then ask a student at random what he or she sees. It prepares the students for future daily routine when they are asked by owners to describe what they see in their animal and what conclusions they can form that will lead to a diagnosis. My problem was that in order to view the slides, the lights in the lecture hall had to be dimmed, which activated a conditioned reflex I had to doze off.

This particular day, though, I had no problem remaining conscious. Before the lecture began, someone sitting close to the projector slipped a slide of their own into the carousel. Partway into the slide show, just as I was beginning to doze, a slide came up on the screen that resulted in an instant burst of long, sustained uproarious laughter that persisted for three minutes. It was a slide of one of our classmates' bare bottom. We had one classmate that had bright-red hair, and all over the rear end before us in living color was red hair, so it was no secret whose best side we were looking at. The professor stood there stone-faced, not even a glimpse of a smile the whole time the class was laughing, and left the slide up for the viewing public. Our lecture hall was next to the dean's office. After the laughter died down, the professor announced matter-of-factly while looking at the screen, "Now we will begin the study of congenital defects." There was another three minutes of raucous laughter as the redhead in the class turned an even deeper shade of red. Just as the laughter died down and the professor was about to continue, the dean put his head in the door at the front of the class and, with an amiable smile, innocently asked, "What's going on in here?" He was greeted by another three minutes of uproar. So ended the pathology lecture of Monday.

Judy's parents were both country and Western music fans. They used to sit at the kitchen table on evenings visiting with each other and listening to the old-style country music. Her father passed away suddenly from a massive heart attack at the age of forty-nine. He was a detective for the Ottawa police, and he looked the part. I would not have wanted to be on the wrong side of the law with him on duty. I often think of him and hope I measure up in being a husband to his daughter. Whenever we go out to dinner here in Arizona, there is often a singer or group singing live to us while dining.

Invariably in these places, the repertoire is the familiar one heard at the kitchen table while Judy was growing up. We always feel the presence of Mary (Judy's mom) at such times.

When I was a student at veterinary college, I was employed for the summer before my last year by the government of New Brunswick. In that province, the large-animal veterinarians were employed by the provincial government in an attempt to defray some of the costs of farming. The farms were spread out all over the province, and much of the land was marginal farmland, making it difficult for pure free enterprise to work in that industry. In any case, I worked with a group of veterinarians, traveling with them to assist, initially, and later, they sent me out on farm calls on my own if they thought it was something I could handle. One such call sent me to a small marginal farm to castrate a boar. My parents-in-law were visiting at the time, so I invited my father-in-law, Mert, to travel with me for the day to see what a day of veterinary medicine involved. He promised to lock me up in a cell when we visited them to see what a day on his job was like. When Judy and I announced we were getting married—Judy was eighteen, and I was twenty-three and going to college and penniless—he wasn't very happy with his daughter's choice or the timing. The fact that I was a Mormon didn't sit very well with him either. Nevertheless, he must have seen a glimmer of hope because he never pulled his revolver or chased me out of town.

As we pulled into the farm, it was midmorning. I was expecting to castrate a thirty-or forty-pound young pig and then be on my way. Mert waited in the car as I parked by the barn and loaded up my instruments and a bottle of anesthesia. The farmer opened the door to a small shed and, pointing, said, "There he is." My heart sank as I looked into the eyes of a six-hundred-pound boar. He didn't look too happy either. I didn't think castrating this fellow was going to have any effect on him at this age and size; nevertheless, I had my orders.

I drew up a syringe full of anesthesia and then rigged a rope loop to the end of a long pole. I slipped the rope into the boar's mouth and twisted it several times to snare his mouth and provide some restraint. At this point, the loud, shrill, deafening squealing began. Also at this point, my hands began to shake. I had the farmer hold the snare while I took the ear of the boar and searched for a vein large enough to insert the needle and administer the anesthesia intravenously. By now the shrill squealing had shattered my nerves and was in the process of shattering my eardrums. I was sure my father-in-law sitting in the car would be getting nervous. Once the boar lay down and the squealing ceased, I knew I had about eight minutes to do my work before he came to.

I quickly jumped in the pen, scrubbed him up with warm water and Betadine, and began the surgery, removing testicles the size of small footballs and tying off the blood vessels feeding them to minimize hemorrhage. Just as I was finishing, he began to wake up. I hurriedly exited the pen, leaving my instruments and pail there. I came out of the shed with one huge testicle in each hand and blood streaming down my arms to my elbows. Mert got out of the car and stared at me in amazement. From that day on, I think he was okay with having me as a son-in-law. And after spending the day driving the countryside with him, I was okay having him as a father-in-law.

I often think of a lecture I received in my last year at the Ontario Veterinary College. It was a short course given to us by an accountant to help us understand a little about the business side of veterinary medicine. I don't remember anything about those lectures because at the time it was all Greek to me. I had my mind focused on one thing, and that was getting out of school and starting to work on some real live patients. The solitary thing that stuck in my mind was this man warning us that when we got out into the field, we would end up working for all different types of veterinarians. He said, "Some of you will work for veterinarians who will brag about never having taken a vacation in many years because they are too busy. They aren't doing anybody a favor, and they shouldn't be bragging. You show me a veterinarian who hasn't taken a vacation in five years, and I'll show you the dumbest SOB in Southern Ontario!" Those were hard words, and we all had a good laugh at the time.

Ten years later, I was that man, except I wasn't bragging about it, and I wasn't in Southern Ontario; I was in central New York. I was a sole practitioner taking care of many dairies. The pharmaceutical salesmen would come by to tell me about new products and would urge me to just leave for a week off. They assured me that my clients would do just fine while I was gone and would just find another vet to take care of their emergencies while I was gone, but I couldn't, in good conscience, leave them to try and find another veterinarian at midnight or early morning to take care of a calving or some other emergency, so I held my post day and night, twenty-four hours a day, 365 days a year for five years until partners joined my practice and I could take a vacation with my young family. Until that time, our vacations consisted of a Sunday afternoon drive in the country to look at a spring where the water came out of the ground into a bathtub. I would gather the family together, and we would take a drive to the "bathtub spring." As I look back, it makes me sad that our "vacations" were so pitiful. Sometimes on a quiet Saturday afternoon, we would take a drive out to the Fly Creek Cider Mill. That was it, and sometimes, even those little excursions were interrupted by an emergency call, and we would head back to the office to saddle up and get back to work. I know as meager as those vacations were, my children still hold a soft spot in their hearts for a trip to Fly Creek. I suppose they have happy memories of family time spent there.

At this stage of my life when I am able to take a day, a week, a month, or several months off, I take issue with my accounting lecture. While I agree that families should take vacations often together, some families just can't manage it, at least for a time, because of financial constraints or, in my case, because of a self-imposed obligation to provide service to clients that honor him with their trust. I would agree, however, that to brag about not taking a vacation in years is not smart. While James was in veterinary college, I had another five-year vacationless period as I was building our now small-animal practice to be able to support two veterinarians. While it saddens me that our family missed out on wonderful vacations together, I make no apologies for those missed opportunities.

One afternoon, I was called to a farm to check a sow that was trying to deliver her little ones. I washed up and passed my arm in to the elbow. I could feel the head of a piglet, but I couldn't get my big hand in far enough to reach behind the ears and provide traction to get it out. Try as I would, no luck. A C-section was out of the question, so I thought for a few minutes, then I told the farmer I would be back in half an hour. Brent and Danny were just getting home from school, so I quickly drove home to get them. They were six and eight years old, had a lot of experience working with animals, weren't afraid to get dirty, and had small hands and arms. They were glad to see me pull in because they loved to ride with me after school.

When I told them my dilemma and that I needed their help to deliver those pigs, they were elated. They quickly put on some old clothes and returned with me to the farm. They scrubbed up and, one by one, reached into the sow up to their shoulders and tried, for all they were worth, to get that piglet out, with me by their side, coaching them. Those are the memories we have that replace vacation memories. We had many wonderful times working together, tending to our neighbors' animals and livelihoods. I'm not sure how our children view those times, but I hope they have memories that are heartwarming and will last a lifetime. As I reflect on those days, my family is an integral part of the memories I have of a busy and growing practice. Or maybe they think of me as the dumbest SOB in central New York. Lately, my son offered a memory of this time of growing up that has been some comfort to me.

When Christmastime came around, we developed a tradition of going to certain farms to play some Christmas carols on our instruments: James and Brent on trombone, Erin and I on trumpet and flügelhorn, and Danny on percussion—usually the triangle. Mallory was just a toddler, but she came along with us anyway, and in her own way, she was the hit of the party. The first time we went, the children were in elementary school, and the last time, they were all in high school.

Our last year took us to a farm in the hills around Cooperstown, where I had gone for many years on farm calls, one or two of our children often riding with me there, usually waiting for me in my truck. When we finished playing our tunes, we visited awhile. The lady of the house started giggling, and then she broke out in an uncontrollable laugh. When she regained her composure, she apologized but said she had to share with Judy and me a story. She said that one morning, she saw my truck parked out across the highway from their house, next to the milk house and barn. She went outside to do some gardening. As she busied herself, she heard something and then realized it was a child's voice coming from across the road, where my truck was parked by the barn, shouting, "Hey, lady!" She looked up, and the two boys, ages four and six, had both their bare bottoms pressed up against the back window of my truck, mooning her.

By the time she finished, both boys, now teenagers, had faces that were beet red, and they knew there was no purpose in denying it. We couldn't have heard their protests above the roar of laughter anyway. I always thought my children liked to ride on farm calls with me. I supposed it was for the subs or pizza we always stopped to get for lunch.

Whenever I saw a family leaving on vacation or listened to their adventures upon their return and even now when I see a family vacationing together, I felt and feel a measure of regret for depriving our family of so many years of that experience.

Lately, I have felt that I may have worked too hard and long without a break and failed my children in that regard. But the other day, our son Danny posted this testament, and his expression was heartwarming and reassuring to me. In any case, there was work to do and bills to be paid, and I did what I had to do.

My son's entry in his journal is as follows:

We weren't unhappy. We had all the land in the world to explore and play on.

Woods and streams and caves and berries and tarred roofs and many times we got to ride with you for the day and all was right in the universe when we were riding with you in the Subaru or Festiva, or the trucks. I'm sure mom got tired of tending to 4 and later 5 children all day every day, but she did so always with a smile on her face and a countenance of love and pure joy. (The wooden spoon hidden in one hand behind her back always at the ready helped too . . . hahaha totally joking). I seriously can't recall one single moment of unhappiness as a child.

Perhaps there were fleeting moments of worldliness that I or we let get the best of us (coming home from school only to see Brent riding around on a brand new bike). Thankfully, you and mom, combined to put forth the most loving and happy childhood I could ever imagine.

Oh my, the stories you could tell if you were to lay out our exploits as your children accompanying you on calls. No one is going to think less of me than they may already, though I can't speak on behalf of all of us. Poor unsuspecting farmers, they never bargained on having to deal with a couple of troublemakers when they phoned in their emergencies and other work to be done. At first, they didn't, anyway. After a few years, I know they prepped for us. Days I'll never forget for as long as I live. Nothing better, in my mind, than growing up amongst the rural farm country of this area. Of course, farms are different than they were then, more corporate entities, than small(ish) family-owned operations. Not to say that it's worse or not as good today, but even as a child, I grew to love the varying farms we frequented. I knew what opportunities each one presented, in terms of mischief and exploring that I could get into. I knew if I was comfortable enough on my own to check out the place, or to accept an invitation into the farmer's home for cookies or some other treat (milkshakes was one of my favorites). I knew which had electric fences that I had to look out for, which had fields that I had driven in, on occasion. Which had kids my age to play with. Had it all filed away in my mind.

None of it, though, ever brought me the joy I felt when I was able to stay by you and watch you work and perhaps be useful enough to help out and fetch things from the truck, or hold a rope supporting the foot of a thousand pound cow or hold a halter fastened to immobilize her head while you worked on them. Lived for those moments. Just us. Somehow feeling like we were leaning on each other to get through the long day. And returning home feeling as though I had been useful And that you'd want me to come along more. Just the crazy things going through this child's mind those days. Just a lovely time and period of my life. Couldn't ask for a better childhood, nor a better family. Wouldn't change a thing.

Charles Francis Adams, grandson of John Adams and son of John Quincy Adams, served in the Massachusetts State Senate, the US Congress, and as an ambassador to Great Britain under Abraham Lincoln. He was a dedicated daily journal writer and passed this trait on to his children.

Henry Brooks, fourth of seven children, followed suit. An entry in Charles's journal after a day with his son reads, "Went fishing with my son, a day wasted."

Henry wrote of that same day, "Went fishing with my father today, the most glorious day of my life."

When I was practicing small-animal medicine solo in Waterville and serving as the bishop of our church, I had a friend who was twenty years my senior. He was a very personable, likable man who grew up in the area, left to go west as a young man and raised a family there, then returned with his wife, after a forty-year absence, to take care of his parents in their old age. After meeting him for the first time, I immediately liked him. He was doing part-time work at the local school as a jack-of-all-trades handyman. His hours there were different from week to week, depending on the tasks at hand, so I invited him to join me as a morning receptionist at our clinic. He was an immediate hit and just what I was looking for.

People coming in the door were greeted by this distinguished gentleman who looked and acted as a father/grandfather. I liked listening in on conversations at his desk as people entered. Often a senior would come in with their dog and give their name. Then he would proceed to ask about their genealogy and ask how this relative or that one was doing, having known them in his youth. Once in a while, a high school chum he hadn't seen in over forty years would come in, and it would be old home week in the lobby. After his parents passed away, he and his wife sold their house and returned to the west. I miss my counselor. He was a caring, conscientious, and careful receptionist. He was a wonderful son and a loving husband and a devoted father. He was my friend.

One afternoon in August, Brent and I traveled to a farm in the Morris, New York, area. It was an excellent dairy farm run by two middle-aged brothers. They were a likable pair and got along very well, so it was always a pleasure to go there.

This particular day, they had a cow with a twisted stomach. She needed surgery, so we prepared to do it right then. I clipped and scrubbed the cow while Brent and the brothers rounded up two bales of hay to act as my surgery table, and Brent rounded up my instruments, fluids, local anesthetic, and needles and syringes I would need. The brothers assisted in restraint of the animal while I injected a line nerve block down her side, long enough for a fourteen-inch incision through the skin and four inches of muscle layers into the abdominal cavity.

The surgery is done while the cow is standing, using local anesthesia. Once inside the abdomen, the arm is inserted into the abdomen, around to the other side to where the abomasum (fourth compartment of the stomach) is displaced. It requires inserting the arm up to the shoulder inside the cow and then pushing the abomasum down and over to the right side where it normally lies, and then suturing the tail end of the stomach to the abdominal wall at the incision site, and then closing her up. It is an impressive surgery, and usually has a fairly large amount of bleeding with a couple of arteries spurting blood out with each pulse of the heart until they can be located and ligated.

All the while, the brothers were standing, watching, laughing, joking, and providing entertainment as I completed the suturing. All went well, and the surgery was uneventful. Brent loaded up my instruments as I went to the milk house to wash up. As I was visiting with them at the sink, Brent limped in, grimacing. The scalpel blade from the surgery pack, although carefully wrapped in foil after the surgery, had somehow poked out through the instrument bag and cut his knee while carrying it out to the truck. He had a three-inch incision on his leg, just below the knee. The brothers thought that was really funny.

I told Brent we could go to the hospital and wait four hours to get him sewn up or he could sit on the tailgate of my truck and I would suture it right then and there. I explained to him that putting in a needle in several places for local anesthesia would hurt as much as just suturing it without a local. He opted for no anesthesia. The brothers stopped laughing. Brent got up on the tailgate, and I prepped his knee and then started the suturing. He grimaced and groaned as the needle passed through the skin, but he never moved a muscle. The brothers by now were getting pale, and they disappeared. I finished suturing then bandaging Brent's knee, and we were off to the next visit. No brothers to be seen anywhere. By five o'clock, Brent was sliding into second base with his knee all bandaged up. Not much keeps a Gilchrist down.

Life in a box stall can be interesting. I was called out to a farm in Vermont on the island of North Hero one evening. I always enjoyed going to the islands in Lake Champlain. There was a road out to them, and they were all interconnected by roads. They were very large in acreage, so once out there, it didn't really seem as though you were on an island, but the drive to them and the cool breeze that always blew off the lake made it a desirable place to labor. This particular evening, my task at hand was to deliver a calf that didn't want to come out. I arrived at the farm at chore time. Two young men were in the process of getting the cows milked for the evening when I arrived. I filled my pail with warm water and got out my calving chains, ropes, and other paraphernalia I would need to do the job.

One of the boys showed me where the cow was and then went back to milking, offering to come running if I needed help. I examined the cow and corrected the malalignment of limbs that was holding up the delivery, placed my calving chains on the calf's front feet, and delivered the calf unassisted. As I was washing up, the young man who helped me told me that if I made my bill up, he would get a check for me before I left. I handed him the bill and watched him walk down to the end of the barn into a box stall. He stood in the stall for a minute or so and then returned, check in hand. As he handed me the check, he smiled and said, "You're probably wondering what's going on. Dad came home drunk three days ago, and my mother won't let him in the house, so he made a bed for himself with bales of straw, and he's been sleeping there for the last three nights." I had to admire the man's ingenuity. I have always remembered this incident and filed it in the back of my mind for future reference.

CHAPTER THREE

Christmas

There is a painting of a Holstein cow and her calf standing in a meadow, on the wall by my desk. When I first started my practice in 1982, I was a sole practitioner for the first five years. Consequently, I never had a night off, a day off, or a holiday nor a vacation for five years. Our idea of vacation was a Sunday afternoon drive in the country for a couple of hours. Most of my work at that time was on large animals, mainly cows and horses. It was a long haul, but I think it was harder on my wife and children than me. To make Christmas different from every other day, I decided that if an emergency came in, I would take care of it and then tell the farmer that there was no charge today, Merry Christmas.

One Christmas evening, a man called with a cow that was having difficulty delivering a calf. This particular man had carried a bill for over a year without paying a dime on it. I was incensed that he would call on this of all days. I got in my truck and went for the cow's sake. The closer I got to his farm, the angrier I got. My steering wheel and dashboard took the brunt of my anger. I decided without much deliberation that I would make an exception to my rule and give him a jim-dandy of a bill when I got done. He was milking when I arrived, so I went to work on the cow without his assistance, which didn't help my humor. I tied her tail to her collar so it was out of my way, put on a shoulder-length sleeve, washed her up, and went in up to my shoulder. The calf was twisted 180 degrees and, in so doing, twisted the whole uterus with it. It was like a cylindrical balloon that was twisted in the middle, constricting the passage way too much to allow delivery of the calf. I had seen hundreds of these deliveries, so I was adept at correcting the torsion.

I put the length of my outstretched hand along the side of the calf's head and began rocking the calf back and forth a couple of times, and then with everything I had from my neck to the tips of my fingers, I rolled the calf over inside the uterus. Once the calf started to rotate, it gathered momentum and rolled all the way over, taking the uterus with it and opening up the passageway fully. That also released twenty gallons of calving fluid in a mighty gush all over my chin, neck, and coveralls, ending up in my boots. Normally, I would have taken that in stride, being relieved that the torsion was reduced and the necessity of a two-hour C-section averted. My feet were cold, so the fluid in my boots being at the cow's body temperature of 102 degrees offered some welcome warmth. Nevertheless, my foul humor was worsened by my sudden bath and drenched coveralls to ride home in. I delivered the calf and made sure he was breathing on his own and coming around nicely.

Then I went to the manger and tied the cow's head up so I could administer some medication IV that would help her pass the placenta and whatever fluid that was left inside. As I stood there in the hay, holding the bottle of fluids and watching it bubble down the IV line and into her jugular vein, I felt something on my knee. I looked down and there was the cutest little beagle puppy, tail wagging, his eyes saying "Pet me, pet me," which I did. Then I looked down the manger, and there was a cat lying on her side, nursing four kittens, and I could hear her purring from where I stood some twenty feet away. Then I looked down the manger, and every cow in the barn had their eyes fixed on me. There was no hate, envy, guile, or malice in their gaze, just wonder at whom I was and what I was doing there. At that moment, a light went off in my soul, and I realized on this Christmas day that a manger was the perfect place for the Savior, the only perfect human to ever walk the earth, to be born. There was no sin in that barn among the animals. They were celestial living beings. No other place among the living could offer Him such sanctity. I came in anger, and I left in humility. When I arrived home, I sat down at the table and made out a bill for the calving. Then I thought of my personal revelation.

Then I thought, *What would the Savior do?* I marked NO CHARGE . . . MERRY CHRISTMAS across the bill and mailed it out the next day. Two weeks later, the farmer came in and paid his bill from the last year in full. I think of that night every Christmas and thank the Lord for my lifetime of experience with His creatures. When I am with them, I am home.

Ricco, our cat, is lying on the bed beside me. In the quiet solitude of our darkened room, his purring lends a peaceful air of contentment—music to calm a troubled soul. He is truly a friend indeed. Johnny One Eye, our beloved rescue cat, is nearby, never wanting to be too far from us. So many three-and four-legged friends over the years. Each has been unique. Each has loved unconditionally. Each has been loved and appreciated. I remember as if it were yesterday my first such friend and companion—Fella. He was an English bulldog. He died when I was five, but his image and character remain vivid in my sixty-two-year-old mind. His broad tongue would cover my whole face. Our mutual love was unparalleled. His faded photo is on my desk. He continues to affect my life. Do these little creatures have a purpose in their existence? Are they heaven-sent? Has my life been immeasurably blessed by my association with them?

No, heaven will not ever heaven be if these, my furry friends, are not there to welcome me.

I went to the clinic tonight to check on things. All was quiet and warm. I sat down in the solitude of the waiting room, the silence a stark contrast to the organized chaos of the daytime routine.

Yesterday, an elderly lady came in with her lab just as I was leaving to go to the dentist. Her dog was my last appointment. She had a chronic ear infection that was still pretty severe. I treated the ears and sent home some medication for the owner to follow up on. I called this evening when all was quiet, to see how my patient was doing. As I was talking with the owner, I could hear a cat purring in the background, so I asked if that was her cat I could hear. We talked about the cat and how she and the dog got along.

Pets really are an important part of people's lives. I believe this lady is very happy in her home directly because of the companionship of her cat and dog. Without them, her life would be very empty. I also believe that my phone call tonight lifted her spirits and gave her a chance to talk about her pets in a more relaxed, less clinical way. She shared with me some things about her pets that were dear to her heart. I find more and more that a sincere, friendly listening ear is a great comfort to many lonely souls out there. Veterinary medicine is so much more than just taking care of animals.

In the late fall of 1978, I was working in my first year as a graduate veterinarian in Northern New York, right on the Canadian border. When the barns are closed up tight for the winter, warm days in the fall breed disaster for a dairy. The barn gets too warm and humid and becomes prime territory for pneumonia in calves and cows. To me it is the most sobering thing I have to deal with. The cows can be okay one day and on death's door the next. Once one cow becomes sick, it's likely to move through the whole dairy. The cows have to be put on antibiotics for at least four to five days, which means their milk must be discarded during that time and for four to five days after until the antibiotics that render their milk unsafe for human consumption are out of their system. That means the farm income goes down the drain during that time, which increases the pressure to get them better.

I remember treating about fifteen cows one evening with IV antibiotic injections and intratracheal injections and coming in the next morning to five dead cows lying in their stalls. Those are times when you must keep your wits, stick to what you know will work if anything can, be steadfast in your course, and reassure the farmer that everything that can possibly be done is being done and that we will work through this and triumph. That fall we had pneumonia outbreaks in fifty or sixty herds. I had a notebook for each farmer where he marked which cows were sick and on treatment, which ones were better and off treatment, when their last treatment was, and twice a day, temperatures of all the cows that were being treated or watched for possible treatment. I would come in and check all the treated cows' lungs and any new suspects and determine who needed to go on treatment and who could come off treatment. We were working late into the night watching over our herds, hoping and praying that they would respond quickly and, most of all, that none would die.

Working through that type of adversity and tension was a great training and proving ground for me. By the time each outbreak was over, we (the farmer and I) were like brothers. On occasion, when the last cow was taken off treatment, we hugged each other. More than once I left a farm with tears streaming down my cheek, relieved and thankful that it was over and that the farmer could resume his livelihood.

One evening I walked into one such barn. The farmer looked pretty pale, so I asked him if he was okay. He confessed judging that the injections we were giving the sick cows were working so well he thought that one might be in order for his bronchitis. So standing in the manger in front of a cow, he dropped his pants and gave himself an injection in the rear end. He must have put it inadvertently in a vein because it knocked him out, and he fell face-first in the manger, unconscious, and with his pants down around his ankles. The whole time he lay there, the cow was licking his rear end with a tongue as rough as coarse sandpaper. When he regained consciousness, there was a softball-sized bleeding abrasion on his rump. I asked him how his cold was doing, to which he replied, "I don't know, my ass hurts so much I can't tell." He managed a sheepish grin, which led me to know that he would be all right. Those days and nights were long and hard, but we persevered and triumphed. It was a time like many others when I could be proud of my profession.

One evening, I received a call from an older woman. Her dog was not doing very well, so I asked her if she would bring him in to the clinic so I could examine him. Forty-five minutes later at about 10:00 PM, she came in with the dog and her son, who was about my age. I was touched that this man would roll out in the middle of the night to take care of his mother and the little dog that meant so much to her. He didn't try to talk her out of coming in nor try to persuade her to wait until morning, he being fully aware of how worried his mother was over her beloved companion. As they left, I told him what a good son he was to take care of his mother that way. I envied him living close enough to her to be able to take care of her. I wished that my own mother was closer—I would love to be able to roll out in the night to take care of her. It is truly a wonderful thing to be able to show gratitude to those that we love for the things that they have done for us by taking care of them in their hour of need.

I have the chills tonight, and it's dark and cold outside. One cold November day in Vermont, I went to a farm for an emergency. It was a cow that had delivered her calf and kept on straining until she pushed the whole calf bed (uterus) out, so it lay in the cold manure behind her, one hundred pounds of engorged, swollen mass that had to be cleaned up and replaced while she lay there straining and doing her best to push back out whatever I replaced. She was down and couldn't get up. In those days I had powerful arms that looked like Popeye's and a few tricks up my sleeve to complete the task, but by the time I got her all back together, I was covered head to toe in cold manure and blood. I went into the milk house, took a spray hose, and sprayed what I could off me. I then got into my car, which had a heater that didn't work, and drove the twenty frigid miles to home, all the time dreaming of my nice hot shower and restoring my lost body heat. I was so cold I was shaking and probably a little shocky.

When I arrived home, I found Judy just finishing her sixth load of laundry. There wasn't a drop of hot water left in the hot-water tank. I took an ice-cold shower, dressed quickly, and got back on the road ready for the next disaster. In spite of days like that, I look back on that time with pride and satisfaction. I was good at what I did, and the farmers I served were close, sympathetic friends who did everything they could to help me complete my task.

We had a mutual respect that came from working together. Those were days I shall never forget and always cherish. I never want to go back there.

CHAPTER FOUR

Arizona!

About fifteen years ago Judy had a series of five surgeries on her shoulder attempting to stabilize the joint, but all of them unsuccessful. After the fourth one, bone was rubbing on bone and the pain was almost unbearable. The fifth and final surgery was to fuse her shoulder with a bone graft and stainless steel plate. Her shoulder since that time has ached without relief day and night. She gets about 2 hours of sleep at a time and takes potent antinflammatories. We tried everything to get some relief for her, but to no avail. Two years ago, we traveled to Las Vegas for a veterinary convention. At its conclusion, we continued on to Arizona to visit my brother. After two days, we discovered that Judy's shoulder pain was gone, and it didn't return until we flew out of Phoenix on our way home. The following year we returned for another week to visit and explore the possibility that her pain would subside. The same thing happened for the whole week that we were there. We decided that it was time to make a career change for me and a habitat change for both of us. We spent the following winter in Arizona, for five months, during which time her pain disappeared.

Last day in New York for a while. Heading for Arizona today. I am excited about what lies ahead; new adventures and above all, relief for Judy. Nevertheless, after 35 years of living and working closely with all of our children, I am feeling a little blue. I took a walk at five thirty this morning from the clinic to home. The road was vacant, there was no wind, the air was crisp, and the sky was black, with the moon shining through the clouds. So peaceful and frozen. I have always loved the cold solitude of late night to early morning winter. As I walked, I said a prayer for each member of my family. The world is a beautiful place, but it can also be cold and cruel and unforgiving. I prayed that they would seek refuge from the evils all around us in places that were lasting and profound. He will gather you with His feathers, and under His wings you will find refuge. Be not afraid; only believe. *(Psalms 91:4; Mark 5:36)*. This is my sermon for today.

Onward and upward. They who are with us are more than they that are with them. To my children and grandchildren, I am with you always. Dad

Judy and I hiked eighteen miles today. Two were to the local fast-food place for eggs and a diet soda, and sixteen were into the Superstition Mountains and up a fantastic ravine. By the time we returned to our truck, it was getting a little cold, and I had a case of the chills. It reminded me of one winter afternoon when I went to check a bunch of cows at a dairy farm in New York. Six cows had twisted stomachs and needed surgery. It was twenty below zero outside and colder inside the barn. Each surgery took forty-five minutes, and I had to strip to the waist to scrub up and operated that way. In between each surgery, I pulled my coat on to prep the next cow and regain some body heat. Before I began the last surgery, I went out to my truck and started it up and cranked the heater and blower up to as high as they would go.

When I finished and dressed again for the last time, my hands were shaking and my whole body vibrating uncontrollably. The cows were doing fine but the doctor was blue. I climbed into my truck and felt the lovely, delicious, heart-and body-warming heat blowing over me like the hot sun in July. It felt so good I almost shed a tear. I think of that day whenever I get chilled and remember my old friend, my truck, with the wonderful heater. It's amazing the simple things that bring us the greatest and most exhilarating joy. Life doesn't have to be so complicated, but it is.

I returned to the clinic to see a few small-animal appointments. I took a short hot shower and then began the appointments. One of them was an eight-ounce chinchilla with a large tumor on his hind leg. I had just operated on six 1,500-pound cows and wrestled all day with cows, horses, farmers, and all manner of large animals, and now my patient weighed less than a cup of coffee. But the owner loved that little creature with all her heart, and that was what brought us together in the exam room.

I had never operated on something so tiny. It needed to have the leg amputated, so general anesthesia was the order of the day. I devised a mask from a plastic syringe cover and made a hole in the bottom into which I could place the tube carrying oxygen blended with gas anesthetic to render the beast unconscious and without pain. We clipped and scrubbed the leg, and I chose the smallest suture materials we had and went into surgery. I carefully dissected the muscles of the leg and ligated all the tiny bleeders and removed the leg. I sutured up the muscles covering the bone that was left and then sutured the skin. I shut off the anesthetic so the chinchilla was just on oxygen, and within five minutes, it was up and moving around.

In an hour, it was eating and doing well. It was the most remarkable thing I had ever done. Such a tiny beating heart about the size of an acorn, but valiant in the struggle to live. It is amazing the effect such a tiny creature can have on a human being. They can uplift, strengthen, give purpose to being, save from depression, exhilarate, and bring joy to the troubled heart. It certainly did all those things for me. As I watched it recover and run around, I felt great purpose in my chosen career as I relayed to the owner the remarkable recovery of her beloved pet and watched her shed tears of relief. Thank you, Lord, for helping me to learn such an art that brings relief from suffering, and joy and comfort to those souls with tender hearts for all thy creatures, large and small.

I went to see the hanging barber two days ago for my monthly shearing. He knows me now. I call him the hanging barber because he has a small one-room shop on the Old West Highway with bars on the windows. There is a front porch with log posts supporting the overhanging roof. There are three pictures on the wall inside, all framed photos of the hanging of Tom "Blackjack" Ketchum on April 26, 1901. The barber is a colorful character who entertains with stories and philosophy on life in general while he does his work. He does a good job. He said he was hoping I would come in after four someday for my haircut so I could meet and visit with his twelve-year-old granddaughter who stopped there on her bicycle every day on her way home from school and spent an hour or so with him at his workplace. I like this little girl already. It tells me something about a child when they like to spend time with the over-the-hill gang.

He says she's very focused on becoming a veterinarian. I can always tell who truly loves animals and who just likes warm and cuddly by how willing they are to clean a dirty cage. Some will just do it when they notice, and some will report that there's a dirty cage that needs cleaning. It is a job I have done countless times. One of the duties I enjoyed and felt the most satisfaction from while working on the dairy farm during my veterinary college days was bedding the cows down after milking, and cleaning and bedding down the calf pens. There is something satisfying, exhilarating, and even peaceful about standing in a clean calf pen, freshly bedded with bright-yellow straw, and watching the calves jump and kick up their feet and rejoice in their fresh surroundings. I miss those days. Today I will stop at the barbershop after four to meet my barber's granddaughter and share with her some things about veterinary medicine that are dear to my heart.

I will know after a few minutes of talking with her if she truly is who her grandfather thinks. From her actions thus far, I am hopeful.

Sunday I wrenched my back, giving the dog a bath. Then my heart started skipping beats. So I hobbled to church and found a spot to sit. In the priesthood meeting, they spoke of an elderly couple that were too sick to come to church anymore and asked us to remember them in our prayers. I got their address and phone number and called them in the evening and introduced myself and asked if I could come over to visit. They had company, so I left it at that. Monday I could hardly get around with my back, and my heart was still skipping beats. Tuesday was a little better, and I went to the temple with my brother in the early morning, then Judy drove me all around sightseeing. Today my heart is strong and steady, and my back is strong again. At 8:00 AM, our doorbell rang, and a little Spanish girl of about five years old stood there all dressed up for school with her backpack over her arm. Her nine-year-old sister waited at the end of the driveway for her. I knelt down on one knee to hear her tiny voice.

She said, "Is there anything I can do for you this afternoon after school?" I asked her to repeat what she said. I was touched by this little angel and her innocence and sincere goodwill. I shook her hand and said, "You've already done a great thing for me. Thank you." She smiled at me and left for school. I thought of the elderly couple I called on Sunday and then forgot about with my own troubles. Today before the sun goes down, I will knock on their door and ask if there is anything I can do for them today. Thank you, Lord, for reminding me. And thank you for the little angel who knocked on my door this morning, for of such is the kingdom of heaven.

This morning, I walked the dog under a clear, starlit Arizona sky. It was quiet and peaceful. Our daughter Mallory and son-in-law Garret depart for Virginia today. Our eldest daughter Erin and husband Corey and their family left two days ago. Judy has been sick all week with bronchitis and a head cold and fever. She was devastated that this happened on this week of all weeks. Bed rest was the order of the day but not for this courageous girl. She didn't want to miss a moment of time with her children and grandchildren. Warning: do not get between this gentlewoman and her children.

Today, she is a little better than yesterday, and tomorrow she will be better than today. To me she is better than she has ever been. I am grateful that I am still her hero. I hope it will ever be thus. We had a wonderful Thanksgiving with family including uncles, cousins, nephews, and grandchildren. All of us have weathered many storms over the years, and yet when we get together, laughter still comes easily. The resiliency of the human soul is comforting and inspiring.

Last night we went out to dinner with uncles, cousins, and nephews. It was a Mexican feast. As we were eating from a table of delicious meals, a young woman and her ten-year-old son came up to our table with a sign handwritten on cardboard telling of their plight and asking for money. The girl was from Romania and spoke broken English in a soft voice, so I had a difficult time understanding her. I asked her son his name, which he repeated two or three times before I got it. I shook his hand and asked him how he was doing. I don't know if they were really destitute, and I'm not a fool, but I would rather part with $20 to a con artist than lie awake all night wondering if I had told someone there was no room at the inn.

I am sorry for that family that such a young man with a twinkle in his eye and a courteous and humble demeanor must be subjected to strangers' scrutiny and distrust as they moved table to table, whether by choice or out of respect for his mother's direction. I am grateful to my own parents who sheltered me and kept the wolves outside the four walls of our house no matter how humble those four walls were. My hat is off to the young boy for going with his mother no matter how he felt about it. His obedience to his mom touched my heart.

I went for a late-night walk through downtown San Diego, where we traveled from Arizona to attend a veterinary conference. The homeless that were on every street corner this morning had, for the most part, found shelter for the night. An occasional one lay asleep on the cold sidewalk with his/her head resting on their suitcase or duffel partly as a pillow and partly to protect it while sleeping.

I wished I had a blanket to cover that sleeping soul and money and hope to give all the destitute I passed in the streets today.

Many impressive high-rises lined my return to the hotel. Several had a security guard manning their desks in the lobby. Most had Christmas decorations surrounding the whole ground floor. I approached one building and noticed a guard standing at a stone counter in front of it, so I stopped to visit with him. He took the graveyard shift and shared his time among several downtown federal buildings including FDA, courthouses, FBI, and other federal agency office high-rises. I told him I had a night watchmen at my clinic back home in New York and of the peace of mind his solitary watch gave me, even as I walked these streets some three thousand miles away. I thanked him for his lonely service, and we parted friends, never to see each other again, and yet I knew where he would be on any given midnight hence. Thank you to all those who watch over us both here and abroad in the lonely hours and diverse places. I'm sorry I take you for granted, but it means you are doing your job and doing it well. May God protect you, and may you include Him in your watch. Peace.

We went to a sewing store yesterday to look at sewing stuff. I can always tell when Judy's shoulders are better when we start looking at materials and quilts and such. When we were home in December-January, Judy had two machines going, sewing blankets for each of Jamie's children who were living with us at the time and sitting patiently at the dining-room table with granddaughters Mikayla and Cady, teaching them how to use the machines to make bows for their hair. She was in her glory, but she paid nightly with intense shoulder pain that persisted nonstop until we landed back in Arizona. For a mother and grandmother, some things override everything else. As a young student my grandchildren's age at a new school, I was given an IQ test. I was in the fourth grade. A week or two later, the school called to tell my mother my score indicated that I was a borderline idiot and would never finish school, and not to expect me to amount to much in life. I remember about that time that she made a bunch of arithmetic and spelling flash cards and coached me after school nightly with them until I went from the bottom of my class to the top. She didn't tell me about the phone call she received about my IQ test until later in life, so I stupidly went on to finish high school, serve a two-year mission to France and Switzerland for my church (where I became fluent in French), finish university, earning a doctorate in veterinary medicine, and serve five years as a bishop for my church. All I have accomplished I owe to a stubborn Irish mother who never gave up on her child.

The side of my face has been on fire for the last week. Today I had a lower molar removed. If it doesn't show, it's gonna go. That hurt like a son of a gun, and I found myself happy that it hurt coming out after all the pain it put me through this past week. Why is it that at the age of sixty-two, when I am so vulnerable with my mouth wide open and sharp instruments pushing very hard against my jaw, do I think of my mother and miss her? I guess I'll always be her Danny boy.

My son Brent and his wife, Lindsay, are visiting for five days, taking a respite from the cold, snowy winds of New York. Brent and I went golfing yesterday with my older brother and his son. We started at 2:30 PM and finished just as darkness fell. We did a lot of waiting at each hole for the group in front of us to finish up, which gave us a chance to visit. After a lifetime of living at opposite sides of the continent, my son and his cousin were grateful for this opportunity to get to know each other. It was a great day. My good friend Bishop Bloss says that you can get to know a person really well after a day of fishing together out on the lake. I agree, and the same is true with our day on the golf course. After a day in the sun, we met up with Judy and Lindsay and the Webers for dinner. By the time we headed for home, it was nine. I realized that it would be too late to call my mother by the time we returned home, since she was running two hours later on eastern time. I thought maybe I would just skip tonight and call her in the morning, but before I signed off the last time, I promised to call today to read her another episode from my book. I am thankful for the miracle of cell phones. My computer was at home, but I had some of the stories recorded on my phone in Facebook, so I borrowed Brent's phone to make the call and read to her a story from my own phone while my brother Mike drove us home. She had taken her phone to bed with her in case I called. I believe I have a new nightly duty, for which I am grateful. After I read and visited with her, I put on the speakerphone for Mike to visit. He had a great visit with her as well, and then we said good night. As I rode along in the truck listening to my older brother visit with our mother, it seemed for a moment that we were all together again, so many years ago, visiting in the living room at the end of the day before retiring to our rooms. It was the high point of my day. Old age is not easy, and often it is heartbreaking, but there are moments that are sweet that don't come by any other route than a long life together serving one another and accepting and making the most of the circumstances as they arise. I will always treasure these times when, after all the years of being a recipient of my mother's grace, I can, in some small way, let her know that all she did became a part of me and who I am. Lightening her load wherever I can is now my sacred duty, which I wholeheartedly embrace. Good night, Mom.

This Sunday morning in Arizona, the sun shone after a two-day absence. It was like a long-lost friend returned. We took a drive in the country toward the snowcapped mountains. The warmth of the sun through the car windows and the beauty of the surroundings said to me, "It's your last Sunday. No one will really miss you if you don't go to church today. Just keep on driving and enjoy this one last Sunday in Arizona out in the countryside you've come to love so much." My father's voice from the past said, "The Lord provided you with this wonderful place and preserved your life to enjoy it. Don't you think four hours out of a whole week to go and spend time in remembrance of all that He has done for you is very little?" My father won out. I am once again grateful that I listened to my father's voice.

As we walked into the church, a young man asked if I would assist with the administration of the sacrament. We listened in the sacrament meeting to the bishop and his daughter sing beautifully and in a peaceful, reassuring way a hymn that addressed all the evil that has happened this week. In Sunday school, we discussed how to live through adversity, and I was asked to give the closing prayer. In the priesthood meeting, I fellowshipped with the men I worked with yesterday to replace a roof on someone's home. Friendships are born through service. I now have some truly great friends here. I shook the hand of the young man whose family's roof we repaired and with whom I worked on the roof yesterday. I asked him if it leaked at all in the downpour last night. He expressed sincere gratitude to me for coming to their assistance.

During our priesthood lesson, four brethren spoke of their experiences during the Vietnam and Korean wars and how they dealt with adversity there. One elderly brother told of his mission to Africa some twelve thousand miles from home many years ago and waking up to find his companion dead. He was all alone for three days before his mission president could be notified and come to his aid. It was a touching account to hear an eighty-five-year-old man tell of being twelve thousand miles from his mother at such a time and how lost he felt but how he was sustained in his duty to his companion.

I sat beside a brother at the start of the priesthood meeting, and we shared a time in our youth. He grew up on a farm but got sick to his stomach every time they slaughtered an animal for food. He was relieved of that duty by his parents because of his sensitivity. He was, however, very adept at judging livestock and won many awards for his expertise. I shared with him that our daughter Erin was a grand champion showman when she was just twelve years old. For some reason, I felt inspired to share with him that on one of my visits to my parents in Ottawa, a man in his fifties was introduced to me by my father. Dad told him I was a veterinarian. The man then shared with me, in the foyer before church, his story. He said when he was twelve or so, he was responsible for taking care of the calves. He left a heat lamp on one night, and the barn caught fire, killing all the animals inside; all the farm machinery and hay were lost. His father was ruined financially and lost the farm and had to struggle financially for a long time before finding a job to provide for his family.

Then I went into church to sit by my parents. His story haunted me all the way through church. After the closing prayer, I sought the man out and took him aside. I said, "Your story got me thinking. I see how affected by what happened you are even now. Let me ask you, do you think those animals are still suffering?" He said no. "Where do you think they are since they are without sin?" "With God, I suppose," he said. "Do you think God is angry with you for what happened?" "No." "Do you think your father still blames you?" "No," he said, "as a matter of fact, he never mentioned it even at the time. He just carried on and never held me to blame." "Well then," I asked, "don't you think it's time you forgave yourself then and forgot about it and got on with your life?"

Two years later on a visit to my parents, I ran into this man at church. He shook my hand and held my shoulder and said, "I have often thought of what you told me a while ago, and I want you to know that it has helped me a great deal." I finished my story, and the man here in Arizona asked me, "How did you know I'm speaking in church in two weeks and my topic is forgiveness? Can I use that story in my talk?" Thanks, Dad, for being with me today and turning me in the right direction.

Return from Arizona

I'm finally getting into being back to work. Yesterday in the middle of a thousand things going on at the clinic, a woman came in with a tiny three-day-old puppy that was the runt of a litter of five. A pug. The puppy was cold, lifeless, and comatose—no veins to draw or access blood and just barely a heartbeat. This case goes to the top of the list, and all other cases are put on hold. We got our body heater out and wrapped the puppy in it. Then we administered oxygen while mixing up some sugar and water and warming up some milk replacer. These young puppies, if they aren't getting any nourishment because they aren't strong enough to compete with their litter mates, develop hypoglycemia and die very quickly. After taking care of the puppy, I went back to the exam room and found her owner in tears and looking very forlorn. I explained to her what was going on and what we were doing to save the puppy. It didn't help. What eased her pain was a hug from me and an assurance that by getting the puppy here right away she did exactly the right thing. Within an hour, the pup was back to normal and looking to be fed again. Life is good. Today.

Hymn today—about speaking kind words to each other to encourage and strengthen.

I had a young man working for me several years ago at our clinic while he was going to high school. He wanted to be a veterinarian and was eager to learn.

Sometimes in his earnest desire he tried to anticipate how I would treat an animal after my exam. He would prepare medications he thought I was going to use before I had made up my mind how to proceed. If I chose a different treatment regime, he would feign exasperation. Once, I came close to speaking sharply to him but stopped short for some reason, realizing that it wasn't critical but rather just a product of fatigue and being busy on my part. He later chose another career path and left our employ on good terms. A month or two later, I received a letter from his mother, thanking me for helping her son through a difficult time. She explained that the other youth at school were singling him out for ridicule and that he was getting counseling because of his low self-esteem. She and her husband were very worried about him, but working at our clinic and being trusted with the tasks we assigned him were a great assistance to him in restoring his self-confidence and self-esteem. After reading her letter, I was a little ashamed of myself but very grateful that I held my tongue. I am grateful for that still, small voice that speaks to us at every hour at home, at work, at play, or at church. I hope I listen.

A day in the life. Awoke at 3:00 AM thinking of a diabetic dog that was on an IV at the clinic that came in two days ago with blood sugar over 600. Blood sugar was down to 300 by nine last night, but the dog was still not eating. I rolled out of bed, dressed, and drove up to the clinic. I was greeted by our night watchman and good friend who watches over all through the lonely midnight to morning hours. The patient's food dish was licked clean, and all was well. Back to bed now to await the start of another intriguing day of veterinary medicine. Maybe I have become an excessive worrier as I've aged, but I remember one night in my thirties when we brought a young dog to bed with us that we were worried about after a difficult surgery in the late hours of the day. In those days, we were alone in the business and had no night person to monitor things. Judy has always been willing and ready to nurture those that needed it, myself often on the list.

I was thinking this afternoon of my tour of the USS *Midway* last month in San Diego. It brings to mind an elderly gentleman who moved into our ward at church a few years ago. He was ninety-five. His wife and son had passed away in Rochester, leaving him alone in all the world. He came to Utica to finish out his years in an assisted living home. His story touched me, and I decided to help him make his last days meaningful. I visited him weekly in his apartment. I learned that as a youngster, he lived on his grandparents' farm in the hills where I practiced. I took him for a drive one afternoon among the hills and valleys that I knew so well until we found his boyhood home. He shared with me on one of my visits that he served on a destroyer in World War II in the North Atlantic searching for German U-boats. One day my parents were visiting from Ottawa. My father patrolled the same area from the air in a Liberator bomber, also searching for German U-boats. I took my dad up to meet my friend. It was a privilege to sit with these two old warriors and listen to them compare notes.

I learned that my friend received word at sea in 1944 that his mother had passed away. He got leave to come home for her funeral, but he was two days too late. A friend and I searched the cemetery in Paris Hill where he told us she was buried. We found the grave site. One Sunday morning, we gathered with him around his mother's grave, some thirty of us or so. We sang a couple of hymns, and then I asked him to tell us a little about his mother before dedicating her grave. It had been some sixty years since her passing, but this ninety-six-year-old brother could not hold back the tears as he told us about who his mother was and how much she meant to him. Then he said a sweet and humble prayer of dedication for his mother, so many years after her passing and after a lifetime of living had gone by. There have been a few times in my life when I felt as though I stood on holy ground and that the veil between the living and the dead was very thin. This was one of those times. A few short months later, I was conducting his funeral and dedicating his final resting place. It was a privilege to know and to serve that old sailor for the short time I knew him. He was a noble man if ever there was one.

Chapter Five

Bishop Gilchrist

In the fall of 1989, I was called to a dairy farm to examine a yearling colt that had been turned out to pasture in the spring with a halter on. As one would normally expect, the colt grew all summer, both his torso and his head. The bones of the skull grew around the halter, which had long ago become too small. The result was a skull that grew around the halter, leaving a two-inch-deep depression wherever the embedded halter rested. The only way to alleviate the pressure of the halter and allow the bone to grow and fill in the depressed areas was to pull it out, which I did after sedating the colt. It was one of the sorriest sights I had seen, but I could almost feel that poor foal's relief as the halter was cut and then yanked out.

I then moved to the dairy barn to work on a couple of cows' feet. I was an expert in this area and enjoyed trimming out an abscess or trimming up an overgrown foot, except the odor that covered my hands and coveralls even after several hand scrubs traveled with me for the rest of the day. Cows' feet are filthy and harbor all kinds of nasty organisms. A hindfoot must be tied up to a hook placed in the beam above her to immobilize it as best one can. Front feet are lifted over one's leg and rested in the lap while trimming proceeds. The cow will always struggle and lean on you, so it's rugged work, but after so many years, I was built and prepared for the task.

This particular day, as I carefully trimmed an infected abscess on the sole of a hindfoot, the cow kicked out at a critical time, and I cut my finger right to the bone with a nice three-inch incision. Blood was everywhere, and the wound was contaminated with manure and abscess material. I washed my finger and wrapped it with bandage material and finished working on the cow's foot and a couple of other ones the farmer had lined up. I then drove back to the clinic, scrubbed up my finger with a surgical iodine scrub, and got out some suture material and a sterile pack of instruments. I unfolded a surgical drape and put my finger through it and then summoned my partner from the treatment room and motioned to my finger and said, "Start sewing." I knew if I gave her time to think about it, she would send me off to the hospital, which I didn't have time for.

I hit the road ten minutes later, all sutured up and heading for my next call, which turned out to be a cow that needed a C-section. I finished the surgery two hours later, and when I removed my surgical gloves, I saw that all the sutures in my finger had come out. So back to the clinic and my partner resutured it. The first time it was numb a little from the fresh cut, but this time, no sirree. I felt every stitch and then some, but I had no time for any local anesthesia, and I probably deserved the pain anyway. I should have had a finger so infected that it would require hospitalization and IV antibiotics, but the Lord had blessed me on this occasion and on many, many others with a good immune system. That finger healed up perfectly and in short order, and I never missed a day or even a minute of work. As I look back on those days, I realize that my life was protected and preserved. There was work for me to do!

How many times have I told my children honesty is the best policy? On Thanksgiving Day in 1981, I was called out to a dairy in Vermont for an emergency. It was a cow that hadn't eaten for a couple of days; her abdomen was bloated, and her eyes were starting to sink into their sockets from dehydration. The farmer knew there was something wrong and that left untreated until tomorrow, it would be too late. He was right. The cow had a twisted stomach, or abomasum which is the fourth and final compartment of the stomach.

There are two types of abomasal displacements. One is on the left side of the rumen and is not life-threatening and can go on for many days without risk to the life of the cow. It causes a depressed appetite with resultant drop in milk production which alerts the dairyman that something is wrong. The other is on the right side and is much more serious and life-threatening, causing cessation of appetite and the appearance of being acutely ill and uncomfortable. On the right side, the dilated abomasum has much more room to move and becomes a torsion. This means that it is displaced and twisted much like a balloon that is twisted in the middle. The blood supply to the wall of the abomasum becomes compromised, and within a few hours, blood clots form in the vessels supplying the tissue, and gangrene of the stomach wall occurs.

It needs surgery to correct, and it needs it right away. Sometimes when the torsion is corrected and the abomasum reduced to its normal position, the blood clots will release to the circulation, and if they hit the heart or brain, it's the end, and the end is sudden.

My oldest son, a veterinarian now, was four years old at the time. He was my assistant that day. As I was completing the surgery, closing up the skin, the cow lay down and died, suddenly and without hope of reversing. The farmer was there helping and understood before we started the seriousness of her condition. We packed up our things and loaded up the truck to head for home. Both my son and I were despondent and discouraged. It is always tough to lose a patient after working so hard to save her. But such is life in the animal kingdom. You do your best, and then Mother Nature takes over.

A week or so later, my son and I were at another farm getting ready to operate on another cow with a displaced abomasum. This one had a left displacement, so she was not in critical condition, just not eating very well. It was a routine surgery that I have done literally five thousand times, so I wasn't worried about the outcome. The farmer and I visited amicably as I prepared the cow for surgery. James was watching and handing me soap and trying to help. Just as I began my incision, his little voice spoke with all innocence, "Hope this one doesn't die, eh, Dad." To which the farmer responded by turning pale and asking in a shaky voice, "Uh, how many of 'em die, Doc?" James and I both learned as we went along.

One hot summer afternoon, I traveled to a farm in the hills around Cooperstown. The farm was owned by a retiree from New York City. He was young and had a young family, so I think he just decided he needed to get his family out of the stress of city life, and farming seemed the stress-free country life of his dreams. It turned out to be a nightmare. Farming is anything but stress-free, and making a living doing it is very tricky even for the most experienced farmer and almost impossible for the novice. I have seen many of these folks quit their jobs in the city and come to the country for the utopia they imagine lies in those beautiful green hills, only to sell out in a couple of short years, broke and disillusioned.

This day, I was there to look at a two-year-old horse that was three-legged lame. It was a luxury they had allowed themselves: a family horse. They may have even named him Trigger or Flicka—I don't remember. I examined the horse while my farmer friend and his children watched. I had sad news. The horse's leg was fractured; this diagnosis carried a death sentence. Only the most valuable race horse would warrant the kind of orthopedic surgery required to repair the fracture, and even at that, healing would carry a very guarded prognosis. I asked my friend discreetly, away from the children, if he would like me to put the horse down. He said no—he would take care of it. I supposed he would shoot it and bury it on the farm. I left and went on with my calls for the day. Three or four weeks later, I was called again to the farm to check a couple of cows. In the course of my labors, I asked how he had made out with the horse. "Oh," he said matter-of-factly, "he's in the freezer." I hadn't counted on that answer at all. I skipped lunch that day.

I was born in Southern Alberta, where both my parents grew up. We moved to Oregon, where my father studied at Oregon State University in Corvallis, Oregon. We finally settled in Ottawa, Canada, where I grew up from the age of eight until I left home at nineteen to serve a mission in France and Switzerland for two years for my church. After graduating from the Ontario Veterinary College in 1978, I worked for a year in Canton, New York, and then three years in St. Albans, Vermont. I then set up my own practice in central New York, not far from Cooperstown. I worked in those hills day and night for many years.

One day, a farmer just outside Cooperstown called with some work that needed doing on his dairy cows. I had never been to his farm before, and it took some doing to find it. It was nestled on a quiet, obscure dirt road in the hills. It was a beautiful location. I met the farmer, and we went to work. He was a likable fellow, and I enjoyed working with him.

After we finished, he invited me to the house to give me a check for my labors. As I stood in his dining room, he said, "I want to show you the reason I called you to come today." He opened the basement door, and written on the back of the stairway was GILCHRIST 1927. I was very surprised but had no explanation for him. I did some research shortly after and found out that my great-great-grandfather's family came from Scotland and settled in that area. I later found an old cemetery about fifteen miles from the farm that had several Gilchrists buried there from the late 1700s. Two gravestones side by side bore the name Daniel Gilchrist. One was the father who died of old age, the other bore the inscription "Daniel Gilchrist, age 5: drowned." I thought as I stood there about how sad a day that must have been, so many years ago, marked only by a long-forgotten headstone, overgrown by brush in an obscure corner of the cemetery. It is remarkable to me that I am directly related to these Gilchrists, separated by only four generations, and that of all the places in the world that we have lived and all the places that I could have settled with my family, I was here in this place where my ancestors began their new life in the new world. What a marvelous, unexpected road my career has led me down.

When I was practicing by myself in our small-animal practice, I was on call twenty-four hours a day for the second time in my career, waiting for four years until our oldest son graduated and came to work for me. In the midst of this, I was called to serve as the bishop of our church. I didn't know how I could possibly do this—care for the sick and needy spiritually and financially, perform marriages and funerals, offer marriage and other counseling, and all the responsibilities that fall on a bishop of a flock of some two hundred active members and another four hundred inactive members, and still take care of the medical and surgical needs and cover emergencies twenty-four hours daily for a busy and growing practice. Nevertheless, I have never shirked a call to serve, so trusting in the God who led me to both of these callings, I forged ahead. I fulfilled both these duties for five years until my release as bishop. It was one of the most rewarding times of my life.

One of my duties was to watch over the sick and less fortunate among us. One of our sisters, a tiny lady, I came to know and regard as both a friend and sister. She had a frail body but a powerful spirit and a strong will to live. She had beautiful tiny, delicate hands, which matched the spirit that went with them. Her body was giving out on her, and she went three times a week for dialysis. Many other problems plagued her physically, and on four different occasions, I thought that I was sitting by her deathbed, but each time, she was able to overcome and return home. She always had a mischievous twinkle in her eye. She loved her children and grandchildren and, in fact, all children. I know for a surety that she would have laid down her life for any one of them if called upon to do so. I loved her as a sister.

After I was released as bishop, she told me that I would always be her bishop, which I was happy to be. I recall on one of my visits to her in the hospital, she was in a lot of pain. I asked her what was hurting, and she said her feet were especially sore. She had diabetes and poor circulation, and I think they were feeling like pins and needles, only much more extreme. I asked her if she would like me to rub them, and she nodded her head. As I sat at her bedside rubbing her feet, I felt once again that I was on holy ground, administering to the needs of an angel. I always came away from our visits feeling a little closer to my Father in heaven. A few short years later found me speaking at her funeral. I have always treasured the years I served as her bishop and the privilege it afforded me to be her friend.

While I was serving as bishop of our church, a number of Mennonite families moved into our area. They sold their farms in Pennsylvania for a good price and moved en masse to central New York, buying up quite a few farms. I love these people. They were my best farmers. They always followed up on treatments I initiated and took excellent care of their cows. They had the best equipment and always had their crops in on time, ensuring optimal nutrition for the animals they cared for so meticulously. They didn't believe in insurance, self-insuring.

One day shortly after moving in, one of them had a young daughter fall from the haymow to the cement manger below, bumping her head. She was taken by helicopter to the Syracuse University Hospital where she underwent emergency surgery to relieve the pressure on her brain caused by intracranial bleeding. I pulled into their farm the next morning to tend to a sick cow. The owner wasn't there, but there were about a dozen of his Mennonite brothers in the barnyard spreading cement that had just been delivered. I learned from one of them that Jake, the owner, had called to cancel the cement so he could go to Syracuse after milking to spend the day with his ailing daughter. His brethren found out about it and told him to tend to his daughter and they would tend to the cement. A lesson on the brotherhood of man.

When we first started up in practice in central New York, we were an easy mark for many people who had long ago lost service from the other veterinary clinics in the area because of long-standing outstanding accounts. One such free enterpriser stopped in at the house during the day when I was out doing farm calls. He told my wife he wanted one tube of mastitis ointment, which we usually sold in a box of twelve for $14. She obliged, and he took out a check to pay her. The bill was $1.50. He asked if he could write the check for $2.50 and have her give him back a dollar so he could buy lunch in town, which she did. The check for $2.50 bounced, which cost me a $10 bank charge. It was worth it to be able to tell that story for so many years—of how we gave him a tube of mastitis ointment, bought him lunch, and paid the bank $10 for the privilege. I told his brother-in-law the story while doing some work at his farm. He said, "Don't feel bad. I felt sorry for him a couple of years ago because he was down-and-out and had no vehicle, so I loaned him my van. Then a couple of weeks later, I was in town, and I saw someone driving that van. I approached them and asked them how they came to be using it. They said they bought it from my brother-in-law!"

After we had been in business a few months, another man called and asked me to come do some work for him. He was a new client, so I felt good about business picking up. I went to the farm and he had me work on six or seven sore-footed cows, which was dirty, hard labor in the hot July weather. Then he asked if I could dehorn some cows for him. I spent most of the afternoon dehorning full-grown cows, which was hard, dirty, sweaty labor. When I finished finally and washed up, he said, "Just send me a bill, I can't pay you anyway." I think about those days sometimes, and it amazes me that people would take advantage of a young man with four children to take care of and a new business to worry about without a second thought. If it had been for an emergency, I would have been more understanding. Neither of them ever paid me, but I learned a valuable lesson: to be as wary of humans as I was of intact bulls or stray dogs. Fortunately, these people were the exception. I had many, many good clients who became good and loyal friends.

When my boys were young, they would travel with me on the road all day. When I stopped to do a farm visit in the late summer and fall, they would take one of the shoulder-length gloves I carried and gather it full of small apples that were often in the pasture at the farms. Then, as we drove down the back roads to the next farm, they would hang out the window of my truck and throw them, trying to hit the next road sign as we passed by doing 50 mph. If they hit one, we all broke out in loud cheering that equaled the uproar stimulated by a touchdown at the Super Bowl. I decided to join in the fun. I tried doing hook shots, throwing the apple over the roof of the truck from the driver's window to the right side of the road. Once in a while I got lucky and hit a sign with a loud *splat* and *clang*. One time, one of the boys threw an apple just as a police car came over the crest of the highway and witnessed the violation. The boys hit the floor of the truck and stayed there for the next twenty minutes. The French say it best regarding this type of entertainment: *On s'amuse*, which means "One amuses one's self."

When I was a young boy, we loved to watch the cowboy shows on TV. They were my heroes. Roy Rogers, Dale Evans, Hopalong Cassidy, the Lone Ranger and Tonto, Gene Autrey, and a host of other cowboy heroes we mimicked with guns and holsters and caps and adventures in the nooks and crannies that surrounded the neighborhood. Each of the shows always had an old cowboy that would give comic relief or give words of wisdom that had a calming effect within the drama.

They always had a whistle when they spoke, which I often tried to imitate but never understood why that was. As I have aged, I've had a few teeth extracted. Over the years, my remaining teeth have shifted in my mouth such that there are spaces developing between my lower incisors. At the age of sixty, I noticed that when I spoke, sometimes there was a whistle in my speech, reminiscent of those aged cowboys of old. So some fifty-five years down the road, I stumbled upon the answer to my question. I guess if you live long enough, you will get the answers to many of your questions.

Farmers often keep hours different from people in the city. Some begin milking early in the morning at 3:00 or 4:00 AM so they can be ready for fieldwork when daylight arrives. Others milk later in the day, which means they milk later in the evening. Some milk three times a day, which means they or their employees are with the cows twenty-four hours a day. One of my clients milked until 2:00 AM. He would often call me at 1:00 or 2:00 AM to let me know he had a cow with mastitis or a sick cow and wondered if it could wait until morning or should I see it now. Of course, by then I was wide awake, and if I waited until morning to see the cow, I would lie awake the rest of the night wondering if the cow was dying and whether or not I should just go and get it done. After the first time, I just went. Almost always, it was a cow that was not very sick and could well have waited a few hours to be tended to; nevertheless, the possibility always existed that she was in dire straits. After the shock of coming out of a deep sleep and getting into a cold truck, the quiet solitude of the drive to the farm was pleasant and peaceful, a contrast to the busy daytime. I could always get two or three hours' sleep in after returning home, so I made the best of it.

One early morning, I was called to another farm for an obvious emergency. Returning home at 4:30 AM, a bright idea came to mind, and I chuckled all the way home. On arrival, I called my midnight caller, knowing that by now he would be in bed and fast asleep. After several rings he answered in a sleepy voice, and I proceeded with a cheerful, up-for-the-day voice and said, "Say, Bob, I was just wondering how that cow I saw the other day with the sore foot is doing?" Rarely in this life justice is served, but when it is, it can be very satisfying.

My son Brent takes care of the snow removal at our clinic. I purchased a truck and plow so we could move snow anytime of day or night in case an emergency needed to get in late at night or early in the morning. Sometimes the parking lot is three feet deep in snow if the wind is blowing. When Brent goes on vacation, the snow-removal duties fall on me. One Sunday, when Brent was away, I planned to visit one of the branches of our church in Oneida and speak for a few minutes during the service. I arose at 4:00 AM and went about my snow-removal duties.

Then I returned home to shower and get dressed for church. I left in good order, wanting to get there half an hour early so I could visit with folks in the lobby before the service. I decided that since I had some extra time, I would try going a shortcut. I was driving the plow truck, so I wasn't worried about getting stuck on back roads.

I got lost. I drove up and down many roads, looking for any familiar sight but to no avail. Church started at ten, and ten found me on a country road, totally lost. I resigned myself to going back to the freeway, which I knew how to get to, then going by the usual route I was familiar with. I would miss church, but I would be there for Sunday school. It was the best I could do. I pulled over to the side of the road to do a U-turn. As I did, a police car drove by me, going the other way. I looked in my rearview mirror and watched him do a U-turn and pull up beside me.

I rolled down the window. "Do you know your safety inspection is three months overdue? That carries a $150 fine," the officer said with disgust. How he saw that on my snow-covered windshield I will never know. I was angry that my son hadn't taken care of that, since I rarely drove the vehicle and he was in it all the time. I explained to the officer that I had just plowed the parking lot at our veterinary clinic and that I was filling in for my son and rarely drove the vehicle, so I hadn't noticed. "Well, there's a muffler shop in town that's open today, so if you go up there now, they can do the inspection, then bring the paperwork back to my office and I'll let you off," he replied as he looked at my suit and tie and asked, "Where are you going anyway?" I replied that I was going to church, but I would skip it and get the inspection done, grateful that he was so kind. "No," he replied. "I don't want you to miss church. You go to church, then get the inspection done, then bring it to my office." I responded sheepishly, "To tell you the truth, I'm lost." He asked me what road my church was on, which I told him. "Follow me, Doc," he responded as he turned his lights and siren on and led me straightaway to the church. I entered just as they were finishing the opening song, so I was able to attend and speak at the meeting. As I sat on the stand at church, I had time to reflect on the events of that morning. My anger at the expired inspection softened as I humbled my thinking and recognized that these events had led me here and on time. I stayed for the three hours of meetings and then went to the muffler shop.

The owner said he was expecting me since the policeman had called twice to see if I had kept my promise. I had the work done, got the directions to the police station, and headed over there, just as my friend was getting into his police car. He said with a surprised tone, "I was getting ready to send the FBI out looking for you." I smiled and handed him the completed inspection and explained that I had a long day at church. He smiled back and asked if I had said a prayer for him. I replied, "Well, His eye is on the sparrow, and I know He watches over me because He sent you today to get me there on time. God bless you, officer." To which he responded, "Have a good day, Doc."

One early morning, I was called out to tend to a cast whethers. That's an old farmer's term referring to a cow that has prolapsed her uterus. It's a tough case, depending on how long the prolapse has been out. Picture one hundred pounds of red, bleeding raw meat with what looks like a bunch of hamburgers attached to it (which are the maternal caruncles—the points of attachment and nutrient exchange between the uterus and the placenta going to the calf). This particular cow's uterus had been out awhile, and she was straining hard to keep it out. The owner of the farm was a soft-spoken, sweet, tiny seventy-five-year-old woman who did chores and milked twice a day with her grandson, who, dedicated farmhand and grandson that he was, was sleeping through this early time of day, emergency or no emergency. I gave the cow an epidural to reduce her straining so we could get the bleeding mass back inside where it belonged. Her owner was struggling valiantly, trying to help as best she could, standing beside me and behind the cow, helping me to push it all back in. Just as we got the last of it pushed in, the cow dropped like a rock, and the whole mass and some more for added pleasure came pouring out of her in an instant. This refined, cultured lady said in a disgusted voice, "That's right, ass wipe, do everything you possibly can to help us." I was choking back tears from holding back my laughter for the rest of the time I was working there that morning. Sometimes people said the exact thing I would have said if I felt I could. The cow survived.

Monday is always a busy day. People usually only call for dire emergencies on Sunday, so on Monday the phone is ringing all morning with owners worried about their pet who hasn't been eating over the weekend or has diarrhea or vomiting, or all three, or some other problem that really needs to be seen that day. I returned to the clinic at four one Monday afternoon from a difficult calving. Appointments started at four, so I quickly took a shower upstairs over the waiting room and changed into clean clothes and began appointments at 4:10 PM.

My sixth appointment of the evening was a small American Eskimo that couldn't stand me or anything I represented. As I reached to check his ear, he struck out, and doggone it, he got me. No matter how careful I am, sometimes they just catch me off guard or reacting slowly. He laid my third finger open about 1½ inches, and it was deep, and it was bleeding nicely. I quickly bandaged up my finger then looked out into the waiting room. It was full of people seated with their pets and patiently waiting their turn. I was on my own, so I retreated to the surgery. I couldn't suture it with one hand, so I was forced to take my surgical staple gun and place six staples from the knuckle to almost the fingernail in the fleshy part of my finger. I wrapped some tape around it and went back to work.

It throbbed all evening as I finished office hours, and if something touched it or bumped it, it really went wild with pain. That night as I lay in bed with my finger still throbbing, I reviewed the events of the day. It was a tough day, but things had gone well, and I was satisfied with the results of the cases I had seen that day. Even my little biter had been taken care of and sent on his way with medications that I was sure would remedy his condition. The owner was very apologetic, but I assured her that it was my own fault, not having been careful enough in my approach. I'm getting older and slower. Ten days later when I removed the staples, I became very aware of the fact that they hurt much more coming out than they did going in. I have been spanked many times in this business, but I keep coming back for more.

I just can't help myself.

In the springtime, it is wonderful to drive around the countryside and see newborn calves, lambs, kids, foals, and all manner of young and their mothers contentedly grazing in lush green pastures. Foals especially are fascinating to watch, transforming rapidly from awkward, gangly, unsteady babies into graceful, playful, long-legged youngsters. As they get a little older, if left untouched, they become a real handful, even dangerous.

I was called out to a farm in August one year for a colt that had tangled with some barbed wire and had a couple of long, deep lacerations on his foreleg. He had been nursing on his mother since his birth in March and had not been touched by human hands. The owners managed to get a rope on his neck after a half-hour rodeo that would have been very entertaining had I not had a long list of other farms spread out over a thirty-mile radius that I had to get to before sundown. I approached the colt very slowly and with great caution. As I got close enough to touch him, he reared up in the air over my head and tried to put his front hooves in my pockets, missing and settling for coming down hard on my rear toe. After about twenty minutes of wrestling with his head and front end, I was able to get a sedative injection in him. Another ten minutes went by before he settled down. I then was able to suture the cuts and bandage the leg. I left them with instructions to keep him quiet for the next two weeks and change the bandage every day. I hoped they wouldn't get killed trying to follow those instructions.

I returned in two weeks to remove the stitches. I planned on being there for an hour or so, remembering the last visit. I drove in the driveway with great apprehension, hoping that no one had been seriously injured after working on that wild colt for the past two weeks. As I got out of my truck, a young girl led the colt up to me with a halter attached to a loose lead. The wild beast just stood there, watching me with interest. As I carefully reached down to remove the bandage, he stood there like a statue. As I removed the stitches one by one, he never flinched. I realized that the terrible injury he sustained two weeks before turned out to be a blessing in disguise. The nursing care that followed transformed this wild, dangerous colt into a wonderful horse-to-be. Sometimes the wildest colts make the best horses, and that is true in our own species.

Sometimes when office hours are moving along smoothly in the middle of the morning or afternoon, everything changes in the blink of an eye as an emergency bursts in through the doors. Often they are in too big a hurry to call ahead, so we have no warning they are coming in. One weekday morning, a young man came in carrying his one-hundred-pound German shepherd. He found him by the roadside in a cold ditch. He was unable to walk, sit up, or even raise his head. We took him right into our treatment room and checked him over. I wasn't sure if trauma, hypothermia, or a spinal cord or brain infection or other central nervous problem was the cause. I started an IV and administered warm fluids to rehydrate and help restore body heat, put him on a forced air body warmer, and added antibiotics IV and anti-inflammatories by the same route. The dog was very unresponsive but still alive. The young man was a hardworking farmer and dedicated to his friend. I gave him a guarded prognosis but said we would keep him hospitalized, run blood work, and medicate him symptomatically.

By the next morning, not much had changed. He had a very hard time just sitting up. I called to report to the owner and said if there wasn't much improvement in the next few hours, we would have to make some tough decisions. After milking, the owner came in to visit his companion. He sat by his cage on the floor for a long time, then arose and said he wanted to get his dog a doughnut. He said he loved them and he was sure it would help. I knew that a doughnut wasn't going to help where twenty-four hours of IV medications and intensive care had failed, but I figured it might help the owner come to grips with the reality of his dog's situation. He returned a few minutes later carrying a doughnut. As he sat by the cage, he fed small pieces of the doughnut bit by bit. I went into an exam room to check another pet. Half an hour later, I looked over at the cage, and our patient was sitting up. His owner left to do chores and returned later in the evening with another doughnut. This time he quickly sat up and moved his tail a little bit.

By morning, he was eating and drinking and able to sit up easily. I invited his owner to take him home with some medication if he could keep him confined to a small room or pen for the next couple of weeks. I called the following Sunday to check on him and was told that he was now stumbling out to the barn with his owner in the morning and slowly improving. A month later, I received a letter thanking me for my interest in their dog's recovery, saying that he was now chasing rabbits and almost back to normal. It was the first time I had ever witnessed the cure of an animal by a doughnut. But I was reminded of a life lesson I had forgotten but witnessed many times: sometimes after all that we can do medically, it takes love to finally tip the scale in our favor. I was moved by the faith and love of the young farmer and rejoiced with him at his faithful friend's recovery.

Working as closely as I did with farmers, I eventually got to know them pretty well. Many of our encounters were over routine matters, with little or no pressure or stress, but there always came times when conditions were more critical or decisions had to be made on the spot when their true character came to the surface. Sometimes it would be frustrating for me, sometimes I would be angered, and sometimes I was moved by the sensitivity of these rugged individuals who carved out their living by the sweat of their brows and by their ingenuity, tenacity, courage, and bullheadedness.

One day I was called to a small forty-cow dairy to check on a cow that wasn't eating very well and had dropped considerably in milk production. If a cow isn't producing milk and can't be fixed to do so, she is at the end of the line and is sold at auction. This particular dairy was always a pleasure to go to. The owner was an elderly man but in good shape. He was amiable and loved animals. His calves and young heifers were well-fed and bedded in immaculate stalls and pens. There was always fresh straw under the cows and clean shavings on the walkways behind them. The air was fresh, and the cows were the picture of contentment. There were always black-and-white barn cats that gathered around him at milking time, waiting for a bowl of milk and the cat food he always gave them. He had them spayed and neutered, and he took as good care of them as he did his cows. He had been in the business his whole life and was a good manager, so financially he was doing very well.

After examining the cow he was worried about, I found out that she was seventeen years old. She looked great, but her udder was in its last stages of production. She had produced many tons of milk over the years. She had been milking for two years since her last calf, and she was not pregnant after many attempts to breed her. I explained to my friend that she had a twisted stomach that would require surgery to correct. Her milk-producing days were over, and she was never going to breed again, so it was time to send her down the road. He shook his head, and said, "No, not this cow. I've milked her all these years, so she's going to finish her life here and be buried on the farm." I looked at him a moment and saw the disappointment and sadness in his eyes. I replied, "Well, if you're going to do that, then I will do the surgery for nothing." Which I did that morning. She recovered quickly and went back to eating very well, but she never produced another drop of milk. About six months later, he came out to the barn to do chores in the early morning and found she had died peacefully in her stall in the night. He buried her after chores on the edge of a meadow at the back of the farm. He was what I call a quiet hero. And I was proud to call him my friend.

On a beautiful sunny June day, I traveled to a beef farm. The order for the day was to castrate ten nine-month-old Texas longhorn bulls. These guys were big, and they were rugged. My four-year-old daughter Mallory traveled with me that day. She loved to ride with me around the countryside and see all the various animals we saw in a day. I had the bulls moved into a large pen with rugged walls made of 2 × 10 planks nailed with about half an inch between each plank, with the walls being about eight feet high, so there was no way they could jump over it. Mallory waited outside the pen and watched through the spaces between the planks. I tranquilized the bulls two at a time, and after they lay down, semiconscious, I put a halter on them and then roped them up to completely immobilize them.

After I removed both testicles, I threw them over the fence, outside of the pen, and then untied the bull and sat him up so he wouldn't bloat. They lay there most of the morning before they came to enough to get up and start walking. By the time we were done, there were ten bulls, now steers, all lying quietly in the pen. I heard Mallory shout "Dad!" from the gate. I looked over to see her standing outside the gate with the testicles all piled neatly at her feet, except for the two she held up, one in each hand, with blood running down her arms to her elbows. I didn't tell her mother that story. A few months later, my parents were visiting us from Canada for a week. Judy and I left them for an afternoon to stay with the children while we ran some errands. My mother was laughing when we returned in the evening. She tucked Mallory in earlier and was turning out the light when Mallory asked, "Grandma, do you like testhticles?" I have no secrets.

Chapter Six

Poochie

A few years ago, I went to a farm for a routine visit. As I walked into the barn with my bag and prepared to check twenty or so cows for pregnancy or infertility, the farmer asked me if I would put their farm dog down. He explained that the dog was fifteen now, and although still getting around okay, he was arthritic and his eyesight and hearing were failing, putting him at risk of being run over by one of the farm machinery. The old dog had come to them a few years back in the night and stayed. He lived in the barn with the cows, so he was with them from sunup to sundown. I agreed but asked if we could do it after we finished working with the cows. I wanted to leave as soon as I put him down because I knew they would be feeling bad, and I wanted the work done first.

The whole time I was checking cows, this dog was at my side. My left hand was at my side while I used my right hand and arm to check the cows. As I checked each cow, I felt this dog's cold nose nudging my left hand, wanting me to pet him. He touched my heart, and by the time I finished with the cows, I just didn't have the heart to put him down. I asked the farmer if I could take the dog home with me. I would give him a home and take care of him. We had a leash law where we lived, so he wouldn't be at risk of being run over, and we had a woodstove that he could lie by, and he would live in our home, all of which would help with his arthritis. My friend loved the dog, so he readily agreed to my offer. That left me with my next dilemma. I needed now to tell Judy that we had a new dog and that he was fifteen years old and that he had spent his life in a barn, so he didn't smell like a rose, and I didn't even know if he was house-trained.

I took him to the clinic, and my technician gave him five baths to help with the first problem. At the end of the day, I drove home to my fate. I should never have misjudged my wife. She has a soft heart, and when I told her my story, she welcomed the dog into our home with open arms. Mallory was just five or six at the time, but I asked her what we should name him. She called him Poochie without hesitation. Poochie was the best friend a man ever had. He would go on an early morning walk with me down a country road before I left for work. Then he would sleep all day by our woodstove. When I arrived home in the evening, he would come to life. He would sniff me over from head to toe. I think my coveralls held scents that brought back many memories from his days on the farm. After dinner and a walk, I would sit in my easy chair, turn on the TV, and fall asleep. Poochie always lay at my feet. At some point, I would awaken and quietly make my way upstairs to bed. No matter how soundly Poochie was sleeping, he would instantly rise up with me and follow me upstairs. He always lay on the floor by my bedside throughout the night.

One night, Poochie asked to go outside, so I opened the door to let him out. It was a cold, windy night, and when I opened the door, a blast of snow and frigid air greeted me. Poochie ambled outside without hesitation. I went back to my easy chair for a few minutes. I fell asleep and awoke two hours later with a start, remembering that I had left poor Poochie out in that blizzard. I ran to the door, hoping he wasn't out there frozen to death. I opened the door, and in he bounded. He gave me an old dog bark, his tail was wagging, and he jumped up at me, trying to lick my face. He wasn't angry with me, just glad to see me. I thanked him for his forgiveness and understanding, knowing that if he were a human, he would have been disgusted with me and probably never would have spoken to me again.

The time finally came when I had to release my friend from his tired old body. I learned a lot from my friend Poochie. He started each day fresh. He was excited about the future and loved me for who I was, never disdaining me for who I wasn't. He loved me unconditionally and I him. He forgave instantly and never held a grudge. He asked for nothing and happily accepted whatever I gave him. He gave me his friendship and loyalty in return. Because of him, I hold a soft spot in my heart for old dogs. I am becoming one.

The Night Shift

I just returned from the clinic. One of my associates took in a dog to surgery. She called to see if I would come give my opinion on what she felt was the problem.

She came freely to the aid of this dog in distress. She had taken the dog in, done blood work, did X-rays and an abdominal ultrasound, trying to make a diagnosis, and then made the decision at 9:30 PM to go into surgery to see if the problem could be corrected. I am proud of our clinic and the people that work there and their dedication, even at the midnight hour. It reminded me of one cold December night Judy was visiting in Ottawa. All the children were away, except for Mallory, who was four years old. The phone rang at midnight with a calving case at a large free-stall barn about forty-five miles away.

Mallory was sound asleep, so I panicked for a moment, trying to decide what to do. I started up my trusty warm truck (by now it was an ancien *ami*, (old friend) taking me so many miles each day on treacherous roads and then seeing me safely home). I took a pillow and some blankets and made a bed in the passenger seat beside me. I then gently carried Mallory, still sound asleep, and placed her in my makeshift bed in the front seat of my old friend. We traveled without sound to the farm. I generally had no trouble staying awake on the journey to my destination, my adrenaline being up a little in anticipation of what kind of a mess I was driving to, some of these calvings being jumbled-up jigsaws of legs and heads and requiring all my skills to sort out. So we finally arrived at the farm, Mallory still in slumberland. I pulled my truck into the free stall so I could keep my eye on it while working. I delivered the calf without too much problem, cleaned up, and returned to the truck and Mallory, still sound asleep. We traveled home in silence, she asleep and me fighting hard not to join her. We arrived home at about 2:30 AM, and I carried her gently to her bed. All this time she never awoke. Oh, to be young, innocent, and oblivious to the world around us. Why do things get so complicated as we get older?

I'm on call Christmas Eve and Christmas. I had a couple of seizure dogs in this evening. I love my clinic most at this time of day. It's very quiet and warm and toasty. I had too many years working out of my truck, mixing IV medications on the tailgate, driving in frigid winds in damp or soaking-wet coveralls with frostbite up to my elbows. The peace and quiet of the waiting room at night come over me like a warm blanket. I love my job. Anyone who called yesterday or today I told to come right in. No sleepless night this year. Everyone was very appreciative of being able to bring in their ailing loved one without hassle. It's satisfying to tell people that if they have a pet, they are never alone. No matter what time or day, if they need help, we are only a phone call away. I feel very good about that assurance we can offer. Tonight I love my job.

When our children were young, we all worked together at home, at school, at work, and at play. One afternoon, someone brought a stray cat in they found by a Dumpster in New Berlin. It was an unspayed black-and-white female. I knew this because she was very pregnant. She also had a mangled front paw, which had been caught in a trap. This I knew because there was a deep compressed line across her foreleg, and everything below that line was ice-cold. Gangrene. She sat purring on my exam table in our homey small clinic. Our children were surrounding the table, and Judy was petting and mothering her. I knew by the look on all their faces that we now owned a cat. Soon to be seven cats. "What are you going to do, Dad?" There come along in life very few opportunities to step up to the plate and be a hero in the eyes of our loved ones. I am grateful for that opportunity and the chance to let that friendly cat know that she had nothing to fear here.

Later that day, I did surgery and removed the gangrenous leg. In two days, she was walking around like nothing had happened. In another week, she was the mother of six black-and-white kittens that could not have been cuter. It still amazes me to watch the resilience of animals. That a cat can undergo an amputation and then deliver a litter of kittens a week later and catch mice and climb a tree with the three remaining limbs and be content in her existence says to me she must know of a surety, something I must accept on faith. In my career, I grew up with my children. We learned together from the wonders that we faced daily. I know that each member of our family has a love for the helpless, be they of whatever species. If I left them with that alone, I am grateful.

A weekend at home

Here I am at my folks' house in Ottawa with my grandson Logan snoring beside me. Today I will work on the list of things Mom prepared for me to do. I went with my dad to get a cabinet from the local lumberyard last night and installed it in their kitchen. I had to saw one-fourth inch off the bottom of it all the way around to make it fit.

My dad, 97 years old, is walking very slowly now and is quite thin. He hardly hears a thing. He still smiles easily, though, and his lion heart beats strong. I got dinner at Swiss Chalet last night and brought it home and served it up to them. Dad blessed it with a short but powerfully moving prayer. Mom, 92 years of age, is very discouraged with life. A deaf, confused husband and the difficulties and dangers of going out in winter are taking their toll on her Irish spirit. But I solved some of her scooter problems, bought and installed the cabinet, suggested she have a nurse come to the house for their blood draws so they didn't have to get a taxi each time, and fed them a delicious chicken dinner. Today I will work down her list of to-dos, taking her to the hairdresser this morning. It is my great privilege to serve these honored pioneers this weekend with all my heart, might, mind, and soul. I love them so.

Everything on Mom's list is done, and I managed to restore her spirits. I loaded up her scooter in my car this afternoon, and we went shopping. Just the two of us. We looked at jackets, and I bought her one, which was a beautiful shade of blue. We tried on several sizes and picked the most becoming. We shopped for groceries and exchanged recipes. She shared that she loves the old man and still sees that dashing young pilot in him and that they still have tender moments. "He just doesn't hear what I'm saying." So I said, "Well, Mom, you can call me anytime, and I'll listen to everything you say. I never pay any attention to it anyway." We both had a good laugh because she knew I was just pulling her Irish leg. It has been a successful visit, and the Irish gleam has returned to her eyes. I love to take her shopping.

On Monday, my ninety-seven-year-old father goes into surgery to get an aneurysm in his chest stabilized with a cuff that will be passed up the femoral artery in his leg to be placed at the site of the aneurysm to strengthen the arterial wall and keep it from bursting and killing him within a few seconds. He decided to have the procedure done so he can go golfing again. He has traveled down a lot of roads over the years and seen the world move from cowboy days and outdoor plumbing to the space age and hermetically sealed indoor plumbing. He is only two generations from the prophet Joseph Smith, his great-grandfather having met and been blessed by my father's longtime hero. During all the time I have known my father, I have never seen him waver in his faith nor in his resolve to live his religion. He has been a loyal, loving, dedicated, lighthearted, compassionate, distinguished, courageous husband and father.

Just last year, at the age of ninety-six, he addressed a congregation of some two hundred men, many of which were just returned from or were on the eve of returning to Iraq and Afghanistan, and counseled with them regarding staying close to their Father in heaven through constant prayer. He explained it was that habit that got him through his years as a bomber pilot in World War II. Last summer, we took him on an epic fishing trip to Cape Breton, which was so refreshing to him—to be able to see and hear and feel the things of nature that he has held so dear and shared so much of with me. Any type of surgery at the age of ninety-seven carries a guarded prognosis. This man is ready to live and continue to experience all that life offers if it be the Lord's will, and he is as ready as any man could ever be if it is time for him to pass through the veil of mortality. For as long as I can remember, he has had a framed poem on his office wall. The poem, High Flight, was written by a pilot of the Canadian Air Force in World War II, Pilot Officer

John Gillespie Magee, Jr. three months before he was killed in a crash. It reads in part:

> I've chased the shouting wind along and flung
> My eager craft through footless halls of air,
> Up, up the long delirious burning blue
> I've topped the wind-swept heights with easy grace,

Flight lieutenant Varge Gilchrist, reporting for duty. Have a safe flight. You've kept your honor bright, and you can guiltless sleep tonight.

Last week when we came to church in Utica after a three-month absence, it was like coming home. So many of our friends welcomed us with open arms and hearts. The brotherhood and sisterhood of the Utica ward is an anchor in my life, one of those things I label priceless. When I walk those halls late at night when the building is empty, I hear the echoes of so many joyous meetings, dinners, dances, service activities, songs, and laughter. Home sweet home.

CHAPTER SEVEN

Quiet Heroes

You never know when you will meet a hero. I went to a farm one afternoon to work on some cows with sore feet. That required hot, sweaty, exhausting labor as the feet are lifted either by brute strength, as is the case with front feet, or with a three-point method to lift and restrain the hindfeet with ropes. As I was working on the feet that hot, humid, stifling afternoon, I listened to the radio that was playing loud enough to be heard over the deafening barn fans that were spinning at their limit to try and create some breathable air movement in the steam bath we were working in. The broadcast was a comedy act. It was a redneck who was talking about his wife and their baby. I was only half-listening as I was concentrating on paring out a nasty abscess on the sole of a hindfoot. He was explaining how he got out of babysitting forever. He had been watching the baby for the day, and when his wife arrived home, she asked how things had gone. He replied that all was well, but "Honey," he said, "you know them Pampers? Well, when they say eight to twelve pounds, you better believe that's all they'll hold." At that point, he had my full attention, and I had to take a break from working on the cow's foot to try and get some oxygen into my lungs; I was laughing so hard. I spent the rest of the day giggling every time I thought of that story, and I probably retold it at every farm I went to for the rest of the week. I wanted them to know why I was giggling.

The next farm I went to that afternoon was a small dairy about five miles down the highway. It was a beautiful road, with many small forty—to sixty-cow dairy farms nestled under large oak trees on large flat pastures with rolling hills on each side of the meadows. I pulled in by the milk house and went into the barn. The hired man was bedding and feeding calves. He had a list of things he needed me to check and do. As we examined the cows and worked our way down his checklist, we visited as was the custom. He related the events of last evening's milking.

Situated across the road from the barn was a small but deep pond. It was in full view from the barn if the end doors were left open. That evening, he had the doors open and a huge barn fan in the middle of the alley to keep the air moving and provide some relief for him and the cows from the heat at the end of the day.

A cow's normal temperature is 102, but when Holstein cows, who are predominantly black, come in off pasture at the end of a hot summer day, more often than not, their temperatures range between 104 and 106, not from being sick but as a result of the heat and sun out on pasture. The hottest place in the county on days like that is standing between two cows at milking time. As he stood in the alleyway, having just changed the milking machines to three new cows and taking a short two-minute break, he looked up and glanced out the door toward the pond across the street. As he looked up, he saw a car at the edge of the pond that had just gone off the road. There was a young teenage girl behind the wheel, and the car was rapidly slipping into the pond and underwater. He dashed across the road to the side of the car. The driver couldn't get the window down because they were electric and the car was dead. The water pressure on the outside of the now half-submerged car prevented the doors being opened.

The young man quickly found a large stone at the side of the pond and pounded feverishly on the passenger's side window until he smashed it out of the way. Then he reached in and grabbed the girl's arm and then her other arm, and with a mighty effort, he pulled her out through the window just as the car slipped under the water and out of sight. If he hadn't happened to glance out the barn door when he did, that car would have slipped unnoticed under the water, and neither it nor the girl would have ever been found. As he told me the story, I couldn't help but feel great admiration for this quick-thinking and courageous young man and exhilaration that he had saved someone's beloved daughter in the thirty seconds to a minute that it took him to observe, react, and act. I regarded him in a whole different light thereafter. There's a hero in everyone, given the right circumstances. That was his day to shine, and he didn't shrink from his destiny.

Sometimes the tiniest animals have the biggest names. Sir Buster MacArthur was a ten-pound shih tzu, but he commanded the mother, father, and son that were his caretakers. They loved that little dog with a love that knew no bounds. He was a nice little dog, lovable and undemanding; nevertheless, if he acted hungry, he was fed the best they had, and if he was feeling under the weather, they brought him immediately in to be checked. They had very little money as was evident by the way they dressed, the car they rode in, and their humble demeanor. In spite of their poverty, they would spare no expense if Sir Buster needed attention. He was thirteen years old when I first started seeing him. He was in congestive heart failure, so we put him on three different medications to help keep fluid from accumulating in his lungs and to help the heart contract more uniformly and with more force. He did very well on his medication, but from time to time, he would develop bronchitis and would need to have his medication adjusted and go on antibiotics.

We kept him going for a few more years, but he finally passed away at home at the age of seventeen. His owners were heartbroken, but they understood that his suffering was over and that we had extended his life considerably by the medication we prescribed and, more importantly, by the love and care they administered continually throughout his struggles. They thanked me profusely for all we had done for Sir Buster and for our concern for him and for them and, most importantly, for our friendship. I had a lump in my throat as they left, knowing I was looking at them for the last time.

A few weeks later, I was summoned to the waiting room. As I came out of the treatment room into the lobby, there was Sir Buster MacArthur's family smiling from ear to ear, with a walking stick the father had cut and peeled and burned into it the name of Sir Buster MacArthur and beside his name, Dan K. Gilchrist, veterinarian. Of all the gifts I have ever received, that stick is the most precious. It was lovingly and carefully chosen and cut from their woods, and the engraving was carefully selected and burned into the wood. For the last six years, it has hung over the door in our treatment room as a constant reminder to me that the best gifts are the ones that come from the heart. "And there came a certain poor widow, and she threw in two mites, which make a farthing. And he called unto him his disciples, and saith unto them, Verily I say unto you, That this poor widow hath cast more in, than all they which have cast into the treasury: For all they did cast in of their abundance; but she of her want did cast in all that she had, even all her living." *Mark 12:42-44.*

Sometimes my children are amused by my caution of heights, flying, roller coasters, hairpin turns, and mountain roads, but I have no desire to prove anything to anyone. I think unless you have stood behind a two thousand-pound heavily shod Belgian mare to do a rectal exam to determine whether or not she is pregnant and have gone in up to your neck to make that determination while the owner stands at her head holding her steady, then don't talk to me about how timid I am and how brave you are. Usually, restraint is wholly inadequate, consisting of two or three bales of hay stacked up to her tail, hoping that if she kicks, her feet will hit the bales of hay before the bottom of your chin. I learned this lesson the hard way. I was called out to a riding stable to check a mare for pregnancy.

She was an older mare and a good trail-riding horse—not too excitable but with a certain amount of spirit. I stacked up the usual three bales of hay and then had the trainer back her up to them. Just as I lifted her tail, she kicked back with both hindfeet, catching me with one hoof at the base of my throat, and with the other right in my chest. She easily cleared the bales of hay to land that grand slam. I never saw it. She lifted me off my feet and into the air, landing about ten feet behind her. I got up spitting blood and feeling pretty tight in my throat. I was afraid she might have damaged my heart or trachea when I tasted the blood in my mouth, but it was coming from my tongue, which I had bitten halfway through in the center of it. The handler's eyes were popping out of his head as he said, "Geez, Doc, I never saw anyone kicked like that and get up again." Another two inches higher and my neck would have snapped like a twig, and a little lower and my heart would have ruptured right where it sat.

Such was my life. New adventures and dangers around every corner, even with the most seemingly menial tasks. I have had many such wake-up calls in my life, made many mistakes, been befriended and betrayed, asked for forgiveness and freely gave it, and had many bitter disappointments. Yet the path ahead has always waited for me to pick myself up, dust myself off, weep a little, hang my head a little, spit a little blood, and then pull myself together, and finally give myself a kick in the rear end, get back on the path, and go forward. Life is not easy, but as long as I have breath, I will continue to move forward as best I can. "Fight on, my men!" says Sir Andrew Barton. "I am hurt, but I am not slain; I'll lay me down and bleed awhile, and then I'll rise to fight again."

In the wintertime, slush, salt, and all manner of filth builds up on my truck and in the wheel wells to such a point that I can't stand it anymore, then it's off to the car wash to power spray everything off and especially the windows so my line of vision is once again clear. On one such night, after all my farm calls and office visits were done, I traveled to the local wash to cleanse my filthy truck. It was so dirty I was ashamed of myself. It was below zero, and the water from the car wash had built up a couple of inches of ice on the floor. When I got out of my truck, my foot slipped out from under me and twisted sideways. I heard something snap in my ankle and then felt sudden excruciating pain. Within minutes, my ankle began to swell inside my boot, to such a degree that I was sure I had broken it. I hobbled around finishing my wash job as best I could, then I drove myself back to the clinic.

I almost had to cut my boot off to get around the swelling. I warmed up our X-ray unit and positioned myself and took two X-rays of my ankle. I found no fracture, but the ankle was definitely sprained and so large that I had to take the felt lining out of a boot and use just the shell to be able to get my foot in it. By now it was midnight and I was exhausted. I fell into bed and drifted off to sleep. The phone woke me up instantly about an hour later. It was a client, Bob, whose farm was nestled at the end of a back road in the hills around Cooperstown, about twenty miles away. He had a cow that couldn't get up, and she was trying to have a calf. I was working by myself in those days, so there was no one to pass the buck to. I looked out the window and watched the freezing rain coming down. The main roads were terrible, and the back roads were like a skating rink in this type of weather. My truck was parked in the garage, which was downstairs under the bedroom.

I got dressed and hopped to the stairway to my truck. Judy was at my side helping me and asking if I couldn't ask him to call another veterinary practice. I really didn't feel I could ask him to do that. He was a loyal client and called often during the daytime, scheduling routine visits and honoring me with his trust and trusting me with his livelihood, so in his hour of need, I didn't want him scrambling to find a new veterinarian at 1:00 AM and on a night when the roads were so bad. Judy understood and did all she could to help me on my way. I went down the stairs the way I had when I was three years old—on my bum. I hobbled into my truck, activated the garage-door opener, and exited the bat cave. I knew that if I went off the road into the ditch, I would be stuck there until someone found me, because I wasn't going to be walking anywhere on that leg. Before I left, I called Bob back and told him of my injury and asked him to watch for me so he could help me into the barn. When I arrived, my friend was there, at the ready, and came out to the truck to meet me. He was a large, rugged man who cut logs all day in between milkings, trying to provide for his family. He smiled at me and thanked me for coming. He helped me to the back of my truck, where I unloaded IV medications and calving supplies into my five-gallon pail, trying to think of everything I would need so I wouldn't have to come back to the truck.

He grabbed my pail and then practically carried me into the barn. Luckily, the cow couldn't get up, so I sat down on a padding of straw behind her, washed her up, put on a plastic sleeve that went to my shoulder, and proceeded to check her. The calf was a little twisted up inside, and by the time I got everything sorted out and had placed my calving chains, one above the ankle on each front leg, I was on my belly stretched out behind her. I attached the stainless steel chains to a rope and had the farmer start pulling while I guided the calf's head through the birth canal to the straw upon which I was by now kneeling. I worked on the calf at my knees for a little while until it started to sneeze and move around and was breathing well on its own. Then I moved to the other end of the cow and tied up her head so I could administer an IV of calcium that would restore what was lost by the sudden flush of milk at calving time. Her drop in blood calcium was why she couldn't get up and, untreated, would eventually leave her comatose or, at best, unable to ever get up again. She was a large cow, so I gave her two 500 ml bottles of 23 percent calcium. I gave it slowly because given too quickly, it can result in cardiac arrest, which is disaster. After finishing, I unhooked my IV and hobbled to the milk house to wash up.

When I was all done, Bob helped me back to the cow, and I gave her some vigorous prodding. Finally she tried to get up. She got halfway up and started to lie down again. I yelled at the top of my lungs and scared her enough to cause adrenaline to do the rest of the job, and up she went, albeit on shaky legs. This part of the visit is the critical part. If the cow doesn't get up right away, she lies there with 1,500 pounds of body weight pushing on the legs she is lying on, cutting off circulation. Sometimes I could be considered abusive to this type of cow, but I would stay for forty-five minutes or more, dragging them out of their stall, moving them from side to side, and even getting them onto a piece of board that we could drag outside with the tractor, to get them off the cement and onto softer ground with better footing. I hated to leave until the cow was up on all four legs and moving around, because a down cow is a dead cow, and the longer they were down, the more likely that they wouldn't make it. Once we had Bob's cow up and the calf doing well, my job was done. It was 2:30 AM. Bob carried me back to my truck, and I left, moving very slowly down the icy road. By 3:30 AM, I was home and getting into bed after a quick shower. Five thirty came too quickly as the phone rang with another emergency. Back on the road again, and that's another story.

Chapter Eight

On the Road and Present Day

Today finds me halfway to a continuing veterinary education in San Diego. I'm going to learn what's new in our field. There are many hours of lectures each day on the newest in treatment and surgery, but the best part is during free time when we wander through the exhibit hall and check out all the new equipment and electronics and get tempted to buy. I spent three and a half hours in the dentist chair this morning before leaving, getting my face drilled on. I feel like I got kicked in the face by a horse. I think I've gone to the dentist and doctor more in this past year than in the preceding forty years. It's great getting older. For so many years I've worried about Judy's and the kids' welfare and just worked through my own illnesses, never having missed a day of work from sickness in thirty-five years. I've been sick but never stayed home because of it. Now going to the doctor or dentist feels like I'm being pampered. I like the attention (as do my canine friends) even when they're sticking needles in my face or drilling holes in my teeth. Still, it's great to be alive and breathing in the bright sunshine of freedom. America is a choice land.

I hope we can be worthy of it.

In the fall of 2012, I traveled to the busy farmers' market in downtown Ottawa to breathe the smells of spices and fresh-baked goods and to view the abundance of produce and handicrafts of the street merchants. I was feeling a little lonely among the crowd as Judy was usually with me when I went there. I saw a lady walking her elderly dog and stopped to talk to her as I knelt to pet her companion.

I asked her age (the dog's). She was ten. I like old dogs; I'm getting to be one. She was a sweet dog, which I knew immediately, and I couldn't help but give her a hug. I told her owner her dog reminded me of an old dog named Poochie I adopted from a farmer while on my rounds as a veterinarian. His name was Spook, but our youngest daughter, Mallory, renamed him Poochie. He was a wonderful friend I cared for during the final years of his life. He died at the age of seventeen. As I walked away, I heard her call me, and I turned back. She asked where my office was because she had just moved to Ottawa and needed a veterinarian. She was a little disappointed when I told her New York, but I said I would give her dog a free exam, which I proceeded to do on the sidewalk as the crowd passed us by. I advised her on how to care for a few health issues I pointed out, and then we parted. Mutual friends who will never see each other again in this life, but both of us enriched from having taken the time to converse. Wherever we roam on God's good earth, we are never alone, are we?

I realized this weekend that our trip to Nova Scotia with Judy, myself, my father, and my older brother taught me something that was for me life changing. I watched my brother Mike whenever we stopped to gas up or eat or set up camp. In each instance, he would strike up a conversation with whoever was nearby. A truck driver transporting a tanker of live fish, a lady who had a high-paying stress-filled job in New York City and came to her home in Nova Scotia from time to time to escape the tension, a former teammate of a famous college basketball player, and many more. He made friends with all of them and, by his interest in their lives, made the world a better place in some small way. I resolved to follow his example, and to date, I have been richly rewarded. Thank you, Mike, for your quiet example and for being my friend. Many years have passed since we played football together with the neighborhood kids in Ottawa, and now after all these years, we get to play again.

June of 2012 found me returning to coastal Massachusetts for a visit. In the summer of '69, I hitchhiked from Ottawa to Boston and then up the coast to the distal end of Cape Cod. I surfed all day and slept in the woods at night. I was by myself and hardly spoke a word the whole month I was gone. The first day of my adventure found me dropped off in a small New England village at 2:00 AM in the rain. There were no other cars at all coming down the road. I was standing in front of an ice cream stand that had a three-foot strip of dry gravel under the overhang where one placed an order. I unrolled my sleeping bag on the strip of dry gravel, rolled up my jacket for a pillow, and fell asleep. I awoke in the morning as preparations were being made inside to open for the day. I suppose they were getting ready to draw straws to see who would have to kick the bum awake under the eave. Today I made my triumphant return no longer penniless and homeless.

Nevertheless, I remember those days as carefree, happy, exciting times. I have been greatly blessed with a healthy mind and body, which to now have never failed me. Thank thee, Lord, for all things great and small and for the breath of life.

4:30 AM and on vacation. There are no calves to deliver and no colicky horses, no cats hit by a car nor dogs with gastric torsions for me to see, and yet here I sit, ready to roll. Old habits die hard.

We went to the air museum in Tucson today, which included a bus ride tour through the military graveyard for some 4,200 planes, whose noses were pointed toward a sky they would never enter again. It was sad. I saw a beautifully restored Liberator bomber, one of which my father piloted in World War II. I thought of a farmer in Cooperstown. His farm was on a dead-end road. He had a small dairy of thirty cows, so he only called once in a while for an emergency. He was a pipe smoker. I love the smell of burning pipe tobacco, so being a nonsmoker, I was able to enjoy a pipe vicariously whenever I went there as he exhaled in my direction. He was an alcoholic, which might have given me cause to criticize had I not known that this gentle, soft-spoken, kindly man was a fighter pilot stationed in the South Pacific during World War II. All his squadron perished one by one but him. He more than earned that quiet spot at the end of the road in the peaceful hills surrounding Cooperstown, but it wasn't enough to erase the things he had seen. I suppose by now my friend is dead and gone, but I will always remember this brave pilot. I hope he has finally found peace.

I was asked to report on my life at twenty-three. At that age, I was just entering veterinary college. I lived in Guelph, Ontario, and was driving a 1956 Dodge that I bought for a buck. Neither front door worked, so I had to roll over the front seat into the back and exit the back door and do the reverse to get in. Police officers loved me. I was engaged to Judy Dean, and I was as broke as I had ever been. I worked on a dairy farm on weekends and summers while going to college. The only thing I had going for me was that I was young and strong and not afraid of hard work. I had a beautiful girlfriend and a clear vision of the future. I owned nothing and had nothing in the bank, but the world was at my feet, and I was happy. Now I have the same girlfriend, I drive a better car, and I have a clear vision of the future. I am older and not as strong, but the world is still at my feet, and I'm happy.

Wintertime presents a whole different gamut of challenges for a large-animal veterinarian than summertime. Inside the truck it's like a sauna bath, with radiant, glorious hot air pouring out of the heater, warming up hypothermic skin and bones and bringing comfort back to the frosted soul. My lab and treatment-preparation table is the tailgate of my truck, where bare hands must mix medications and prepare IVs, assemble calving equipment, and prepare for the duties inside while the frigid north wind blows, often with driving snow, rapidly biting the skin of my hands and arms with frost and giving me an ice cream headache. Once inside the barn, at least I am out of the wind, but often the temperature isn't much warmer than outside. Sometimes, on a short visit, I leave my truck running with the heater going full blast to welcome me back with the kiss of warmth. Then on to my next visit. Little wonder that when spring comes, I feel born again, having done little more than just survive for the winter months.

One February deep-freeze day, I entered a barn with the shivers. I was chilled to the bone from my last call, and my truck heater hadn't succeeded in reversing my hypothermia. My feet were cold, my hands were freezing, and so were all points in between. My assignment this day was to check some cows for pregnancy and infertility. With large animals, we have a definite advantage over small animals and humans in that we can palpate the reproductive organs easily and determine quickly if there is a pregnancy or problems with the uterus and ovaries. To do this assessment, we don a plastic glove and sleeve that covers our arm up to the shoulder. Then we do a rectal exam on each cow, palpating to find normal and abnormal. The exam requires passing the arm rectally up to well above the elbow in order to find what we need to find. The other day I was checking a dog's prostate with my forefinger (yes, it was in a glove). He was resisting and trying to escape, and the owner was having a tough time watching, so I told him that his dog should feel lucky; if he was a bovine, I would be going in up to my shoulder.

His master wasn't amused. Anyway, on this particular cold February day, I was deriving great comfort in warming my left hand checking cows whose body temperatures ranged 102-103. I felt a nudging at my leg and jumped back a foot when I looked down and saw a full-grown turkey, a Tom, the farmer had found as a poult in the wild and raised as a pet, pushing against my leg. He walked the length of the barn with me as I checked cows, pushing his chest against my leg. I hesitantly put my hand on his head, which he seemed to like, so I kept stroking his head as I moved along checking the cows, and he loved it. I made a turkey friend.

His normal body temperature was 107.5, and his bald head felt like it was on fire, so my right hand was loving the warmth. It was an interesting therapy, my left hand being warmed by bovine rectal exams and my right hand by a turkey head. Such a distinguished career.

What is it about the open road that excites me so? Adventure around every turn. Especially if you're a large-animal veterinarian. I still miss being out on the road all day and half the night. Each day started out at the crack of dawn or earlier.

Invariably, I was able to witness a beautiful sunrise that inspired me and filled me with hope that today, I would be able to complete my farm calls and return to my family in the early afternoon to spend some time with them. Invariably, sunset saw me still out on the road witnessing nature's beauty, albeit alone. For most of the day I was alone, but I was never lonely. One of the wonderful things about life on the road was the time I had to myself, driving from my last farm visit to the next one. Sometimes the drive would take a half hour or more. I made wonderful, intelligent, progressive conversation with myself. Me and myself never disagree and are always on the same wavelength. I also carried on conversation with my Maker. By contrast, there was always something to answer for or apologize and ask forgiveness for with those exchanges, but I never felt threatened or belittled or unforgiven, and always I felt His arm around my shoulder inspiring me, consoling me, reminding me, and loving me. That association made me a better person, a better father, a better husband, and a far better veterinarian than I could ever have been on my own. I felt, and still feel, promptings on how to proceed in a difficult situation, sometimes to call a client and apologize for not being as sympathetic or careful with their pet as I should have been in retrospect. If a visit went badly (perhaps their pet was aggressive and I had to use physical restraint to complete my job), a call in the evening to speak quietly, not under duress, with the owner and reassure him/her that their pet was just frightened and in a situation that he hadn't anticipated left them with a better feeling about their visit.

Sometimes I would wonder how to proceed on a case, and then a plan of action would come to mind, and onward we would go. In this business, you never know what to expect, and a joyful, pleasant day can turn to stress and disaster in the blinking of an eye.

One evening at dinnertime, I was called to a calving when we lived in northern Vermont. The farm was a few miles away from the farm I was leaving, so I headed down the highway in haste. I came around a turn in the road, and there were two young boys at the side of the road in front of their house, visiting. Just as I rounded the turn, two beagles darted out from the boys, chasing each other playfully. They were about the distance between my two front tires apart, and they ran right in front of my truck, which was going 40 mph. I couldn't swerve without hitting the boys, so I held on to keep the truck going straight ahead and hit each dog simultaneously with both front tires, killing them instantly right in front of the boys. I pulled over and ran back to check on the dogs, but both were dead. Then I faced the boys, who were in hysterics, and explained to them that I had zero time to react. They were country boys and had been through this before, and although they were brokenhearted, they understood my predicament and my choice and freely forgave me, for which I was grateful.

I picked up the dogs carefully and loaded them into my truck and promised them I would take care of their burial. I knocked on the neighbor's door and explained what happened and left him my contact information in case the owners wanted to contact me. Then I was off to take care of my calving. No time to feel sorry for myself or pause to get myself together; there was an emergency to take care of, waiting for me to solve. If I felt at any one time in my career, in the early hours of the morning or in the lonely midnight hour, that I was all alone out there on the road, despair would have been my constant companion. Instead, I was excited, honored, and grateful to be a part of a profession that let me pour my heart and soul into my work and deal with pure innocence day by day and hour by hour and feel inspired even in the trials that came daily. As the hard long days drew to an end, I often found myself singing in a loud voice one or another of my favorite church hymns in the solitude of my beloved truck traveling homeward, feeling uplifted at the close of day.

My folks are preparing to move from their home that they and we have occupied since 1962. It was the home I left to go to France and Switzerland on a mission for two years. It was the place I dreamed about the whole time I was gone. It was the refuge I had from the outside world during my most vulnerable years. When I was hitchhiking three thousand miles from home or in the dead of winter standing on Highway 401 at 2:00 AM just outside Toronto, with frigid winds biting my face and my thumb held out looking for a ride, the thought of my warm bed and the smiling faces of my parents at home kept me company in the solitude of the arctic tundra blowing around me. Each time I traveled home, I sat in the living room of their home and reviewed the familiar wall hangings and figurines in the china cabinet in their living room. I walked the hallway and read the titles of the books in Dad's study. Each item carries a memory—some from a few years ago, others from my early childhood.

This weekend, acting on orders from my mother, I brought a few of those memories home with me. They seemed out of place in my own home. Not as meaningful as they were in their place where Mom carefully placed them and where they rested undisturbed for half a century. One item is a figurine from a favorite novel of my mother's. For years, my mother spoke to us of stories from *Anne of Green Gables*. The story has a special meaning to her, having lived in Prince Edward Island early in her marriage.

One summer a few years ago, she and Dad made a trip back there and looked up some old friends from World War II. They toured the island and enjoyed all it had to offer, including a visit to Avonlea where the story was set. While there, they toured a small factory where these figurines were being made and hand painted. When she returned, she told us of their visit and of the figurine she fell in love with, but of course, she said it was far too expensive for her to buy. I could tell by the expression on her face and by her love of the story of Anne that she loved that china memory. Later in the month while driving around the countryside on farm calls, I thought about her recollections of her visit to the island after a fifty-year absence, and I devised a plan. Judy found the place where the figurines were produced and spoke to the artist/owner. She explained that we wanted to surprise my mother with it. The artist explained that she was coming to Ottawa on a business trip and could bring one with her, which I readily agreed with. Judy's sister Nancy agreed to meet her at her hotel and pick it up and hold it for us until we were in Ottawa and could pick it up. On Christmas morning, we gave my mother her present, all wrapped up in a gift bag. She slowly and carefully opened the gift, and when she looked inside the bag and saw what it was, she quickly closed the bag again and burst into tears. I knew she loved it by her description, but I didn't anticipate her emotional response to our gift. It wasn't just the gift that moved her so but also that we had listened to her story and realized how moved she was by the figurine. It was the last thing in the world that she expected to find in our wrapped offering. Now, as I look at it, I see in it the childhood memories of my mother, and I remember her reaction to our gift. It was a moving Christmas morning for both her and us, and one I would never forget. It's a hard thing to package up a lifetime of memories and move on, especially at the age of ninety-two and ninety-seven.

Last Saturday night, I dragged my dad out of the house to have a campfire with me. He was ambivalent about coming; I don't think he remembered what a campfire was. He stared at the fire for a long time, interspersed with worrying aloud about putting it completely out before we left. When I stood to leave, he leaped up and was ready to go. He likes the known entities in his life now, and outside of them, he is very insecure. That's okay, though; we still enjoyed each other's company, and he trusts my judgment and is willing to accompany me wherever I go. In some ways, our roles are reversed from fifty-five years ago when I was much the same as he is now and he was as I am. To every thing there is a season and a time to every purpose under heaven. That which hath been is now, and that which is to be hath already been. There is nothing new under the sun. *(Eccl.3:1,15)*.

Three years ago, we visited Mallory and her friends at Southern Virginia University for a week. We camped in our trailer at a local campground. One Sunday evening, we went back to our campsite. Mallory, et. al., were off doing something, so we retired to our spot. I was feeling a little lonely, just Judy and I, after spending the day with her college friends, laughing and enjoying their young, exuberant spirits. I started a campfire and was watching the flickering flames and enjoying the smoke when they all pulled in to our site. They were laughing and full of life, and I was flattered that they chose to come sit by the fire with us and share their evening with the elderly. As we sat there, a silence arose and we enjoyed the crackling fire. I invited each of them in turn to share something about themselves with us. I began by telling a story about my dad.

One year just before Thanksgiving, he called my sister up and said, "Your mother and I are getting a divorce. I don't want to talk about it, and there is no turning back, I'm just calling you to let you know." My sister said, "C'mon, Dad, you two have been married forever, what are you talking about? Don't do anything rash, let's talk about it. I'm going to call Mike [our older brother] and have him call you." She hung up, and within the hour, Mike was calling. "Dad, what is this nonsense I hear about you and Mom getting a divorce?" My dad repeated, "I don't want to talk about it, I just called to let you know. There is no use discussing anything, it's going to happen, so just accept it." My brother replied, "OK, don't do anything. We're getting on the plane, and we'll be there tomorrow. There has to be some way we can work this out. You have to let us try to reconcile things between you two. I'll see you tomorrow." After he hung up, my father yelled to my mother, "OK, honey, the kids are all coming home for Thanksgiving, and this year they are paying their own way!"

One of the boys shared his story, but this one was true. He said it was Christmastime, and all the family was assembled in the living room having an uproar of laughter and reminiscing. His parents were upstairs discussing some sobering issues regarding their children that they needed to discuss with the family as a whole. They decided how they were going to make their presentation and then descended the stairs. They made several attempts to get everyone under control and get their undivided attention but to no avail. So his dad yelled out at the top of his lungs, "Your mother and I are getting a divorce," which, of course, they were not, but the whole room fell suddenly silent as everyone's smiles and laughter became instantly sober. Without blinking an eye, his six-year-old sister piped up, "I'm living with Mom." Suffer the little ones to come unto me, for of such is the kingdom of heaven.

On Vacation

Yesterday, we went to see an estate, which had a castle perched on top of a mountain, with terraces overlooking Lake Winnipesaukee. The view was stupendous, and the estate was unimaginable. It included over 6,500 acres of land.

It is amazing the scope of things in days gone by. There were one thousand workers hired at the turn of the century to develop this estate and build the castle. Also on the estate was a stable full of horses. They boasted a giant horse weighing over three thousand pounds. He was a Belgian gelding, and I checked him out. There was a bunch of girls oohing and aahing over him and a couple of guys flexing their muscles around him, so I looked from a distance. He was magnificent and certainly deserved the foolish admiration and then some going on around him.

I was called out to geld just such a horse one time. He stood four feet higher than me, and he suspected what I was up to, so he wasn't too receptive when I stepped up to his neck to give him a needle in the jugular and rope him down to do the job. I gave him an IV tranquilizer first while he reared up and tried to kick me in the head a couple of times. After about a minute, his head drooped down to my height, and then I gave him an IV anesthetic. Just about the time I withdrew the needle from his jugular, he staggered and almost crushed my foot before dropping with a thunderous crash that registered 6.0 on the rectal scale to the ground, on his side, and unconscious.

For about five minutes. That gave me just about enough time to rope his foot up to a rope I had previously tied around his neck. That got his leg out of the way enough for me to scrub up his scrotum, sterilize the surgical field, and castrate him, or in other words, neuter him. About that time he was starting to feel things, so I had to work fast, loosening the rope and untying the one around his neck, leaving his halter on with a lead shank attached to it. In a few moments, he struggled to get up, and I stayed on his head to steady him. His legs were going everywhere for a long few moments as I was dancing right along with him to keep from being crushed. Finally he stood up and stayed in one spot for a while, getting his bearings and balance. Then he began to walk slowly and hesitantly, with me still on his halter, steadying him. Soon he was walking normally, and I turned him over to his owner.

My next visit was to a free-stall barn that had 150 cows that needed to be vaccinated against infectious bovine rhinotracheitis, an infectious respiratory virus in cows that could spread through a herd like wildfire and cause pneumonia, abortion, and death. The vaccine we were using at the time was a modified live virus and had to be given up the nostrils of each cow by yours truly. The farmer had arranged an alleyway of steel gates, fastened together and high enough that the cows could only go in one direction with him behind them, pushing them forward toward me, who stood facing them as they came forward. As each cow approached apprehensively, I had to reach down and grab them by the nostrils, a finger in each nostril with my left hand, elevate their head up above mine with their nose pointing upward, and administer the drops of vaccine into each nostril, and then let them pass as I faced the next victim. As I look back now, I realize that I could have been crushed by a panicking cow or trampled by a stampede if they all panicked, but in those days, I was tough and rugged with arms like a linebacker and shoulders and a neck to match, and I was invincible. One hundred fifty cows later, I walked out of the barn and went for lunch then moved onto the next farm for whatever they had to throw at me next.

Sometimes it would be an abdominal surgery, where I would be covered with blood up to my shoulder as I reached into the cow's abdomen to my neck to correct whatever was malfunctioning, or other times it would be a calving, where I would be drenched in fetal amniotic fluid, cow urine, and manure all down my side and sometimes into my mouth. Such a glamorous job was mine. In spite of everything, I loved my work, and I faced each task as a challenge to meet and conquer.

Whenever I go on vacation, my body relaxes and my mind reverts back to its younger days, and sometimes I even get a little mischievous. As a young boy, I held great admiration for my childhood heroes, cowboys every one. I still love these heroes from my past, and I have always wanted to be a cowboy. My kids are amused when I put on some cowboy boots or a Stetson, but I think I've earned the right to call myself a cowboy. If I'm not one, after all the things I've been through with cows and all the stuff I've been covered in from them, then nobody is.

Another busy day at the Waterville Veterinary Clinic. There wasn't an idle moment for four doctors all morning. Plenty of difficult surgeries and interesting appointments mingled with face lickers and heartwarming puppies, kittens, cats, and older dogs alike, each with their endearing charms. In a moment when one exam room emptied and was awaiting the next appointment to enter, I sat down at our desk to look at the phone messages. One caught my eye because it looked like someone just needed a quick question answered about diet, so I dialed and listened. It was an elderly lady and her friend or daughter who lived together in the backwoods about fifteen miles south of us. She wanted to know if we could provide her with a diet her dog was on. "Sure," I replied, "we do deliveries twice a week, and our delivery man can drop it off tomorrow." She was thrilled because she was losing her sight and had taken her car off the road this past week and didn't know how she was going to get this special diet her dog was on. I assumed it was one of the prescription diets we carried for all sorts of medical requirements. I asked which diet she needed, and she told me it was a major brand name and that it was sold at Pet Smart.

By then, after all her raving about what a wonderful delivery service we had, I wondered how to tell her that our deliveries were of the food and medications we carried—not just anything. I paused for a moment, reviewing in my mind the schedule for my afternoon off that I had carefully planned out. How could I disappoint a blind, elderly, down-on-her-luck lady? So I asked what the brand and type of food it was and what size bag she wanted.

At the end of morning office hours, I went home and flopped on the couch and slept hard for an hour. When I awoke, I sat at my desk and paid some bills. I went out to the garage and tried to start the Chevy, and then I headed north to Utica and picked up her dog food at Pet Smart, then back again thirty miles south to the back roads. Fortunately, we had a GPS in our truck, and it took me straight to her house, which was on a seasonal road in the hills of Brookfield, and her driveway was an uphill grass-covered path to her small mobile home. I also brought a rabies vaccination for her dog.

It reminded me of a time I went to check some cows at a farm around Morris, New York. The farmer was a middle-aged man who had somehow lost one arm at some point in his life, but he made out fine milking and doing chores and driving the tractor with what he had. I exited my truck by the milk house, and he came out to greet me, swearing because he tried to call and speak to me before I came to see if I would stop at the store on my way and pick up a pack of cigarettes for him. Groceries—yeah, I would do that, but cigarettes—no, I don't think so. So such is my life. One minute performing delicate surgery on the urethra of a cat or the eyelid of a trusted family dog, and the next delivering dog food and groceries. It's not hard to stay humble in this field. But I wouldn't change a thing. It's good to feel useful.

I was called to a farm one Sunday afternoon to check a down cow. I arrived at the barn and got my medications and equipment together and got on the farm tractor with my client. We drove over a bumpy trail about a half mile to the edge of a stream that ran through the farm. Then we disembarked and started walking up the side of the stream. There were steep cliffs on either side of the stream as we proceeded upstream another half mile until we came upon the cow at the edge of the stream and at the bottom of a cliff. I wasn't sure if she had gone down there with milk fever or if she had fallen over the cliff and injured her back or pelvis. There was no doing X-rays out here in the middle of nowhere, so I decided to treat her for hypocalcemia and see what would happen. As it turned out, she got up after I gave her some calcium intravenously, so we chased her back toward the barn, and then my farmer took me on a hike farther upstream to a most beautiful waterfall, only much wider with a large pool at the bottom. It was secluded by the woods around it at the top, and I had driven close by it many times on a dirt road a quarter mile east of it and never knew this beautiful scene existed. I stood there in awe and just took in this incredible scene for quite a while before my friend broke my trance and headed me back to the barn and reality. It's good to step out of the lonely, dreary world once in a while into the fantasy world of Mother Nature. I think of that visit from time to time and the welcome respite I had from a busy, stressful day. It was a few welcome moments away from speeding down the road to my next farm call, trying to finish my day's work and effect the recovery of so many sick creatures.

This week, I stayed home and took care of business. After working in Oneida last month, cleaning out basements after the flood, I talked it over with Judy, and we both had the firm resolve to clean out our own basement before we had to, and we didn't stop there. We cleaned out our garage and storage shed, and I decluttered and cleaned out my office. I felt like a new man. We were ruthless in our duties, and many visualizations of memories went down the road but not out of our hearts and minds. My friend said it best when they were preparing to move to Europe and sorting through things. Stuff can really tie you down and reduce your freedom. It's good to travel light as you get older and be prepared to move on. At least from my perspective. I started hauling things down to the roadside as Judy sorted through it all and okayed the items to go. Once a month, the town picked up whatever you put by the roadside. Or so I thought. After I had a pile by the road, a town worker stopped to tell me that the policy had changed and things had to be organized into categories and put into containers before they would be picked up. I decided it was time to rent a Dumpster and skip the town pickup, but I left everything by the road for the time being.

By evening, everything I had put out was gone. People passing by stopped and took whatever they could use. So I continued bringing things out to the road. There were tons of things that had sat in our basement unused for years. One item took me and two other men to lift and carry down to the road, and within two hours, two guys and a pickup truck stopped and picked it up. An old shed I had used as a lean-to for a nativity scene in the yard that was made for me by the people up the road making sheds was in pieces in my garage. Each piece weighed over a hundred pounds, so I had to drag them one by one down to the road and lean them against the giant oak tree at the end of the driveway at midnight one night. By noon the next day, they were all gone. I was amazed at all the things I had been tripping over all these years leaving with such ease. I started taking Judy's purses and china and furniture down. I couldn't stop myself, but Judy did.

We also loaded up a Dumpster with other things we deemed unusable such as papers, broken items, etc. My grandchildren stopped by with their parents for a swim and looked into the Dumpster to see what we were discarding. Soon they were in the Dumpster pulling out things they could use. It was like a treasure hunt. Christmas in August right in our driveway. We laughed and were excited that they could use what we thought was junk. After three days and nights of cleaning out our buildings, Judy and I were exhausted but exhilarated. I was amazed at how many things were gone, if left by the roadside, and happy that someone was able to use them. If I spotted someone taking an item, I walked down to talk to them and tell them a story about what they were taking and wish them well.

While I was in college, I worked weekends and summers on a dairy farm near Fergus, Ontario. The summer days were hot and humid and long. The days found me out in the fields making hay, spreading manure, fixing and building fences, cutting fence posts from a cedar forest, and all manner of outside farmwork that had to be done between milking times at 5:00 AM and 5:00 PM. As I did my work out in the solitude of a back pasture or the deep woods or along a lonely fence line, I was tempted to take off my shirt and let off some body heat and absorb some sun into my bleached white Irish torso. I never gave in to that temptation, so I had what I call a farmer's tan, from my neck up and my midarms down. If I didn't take off my shirt, you would have thought I was a California boy.

Later, when I was in my early forties, I was running my own dairy practice in central New York. I had a client my own age, who became a good friend of mine. He was an uncomplicated man, always smiling and always cheerful even in the face of adversity, which he faced daily. I always enjoyed going to work at his farm. He and his wife had six wonderful children, who helped out daily at the barn, and all of them were always cheerful. In the milk house, they had a picture of a mule's head lifted skyward in a joyous way, with his lips open showing his teeth in a friendly way that was very funny. Under it on the picture were the words "AW HORTH THIT." It became my saying when things got complicated and I started to take myself or others too seriously. They all had bright-red hair and a skin complexion similar to my own. He worked outside all summer with his shirt off. He had a handsome suntanned face.

One day when I was doing some work there, he told me he had a sore on his back that wouldn't heal, so he was going to the doctor to have it checked. A few weeks later, I was again at the farm to check some cows, and he told me in the course of our work that they told him that the growth on his back had been removed and biopsied, and it was a malignant melanoma. One year later, he departed this world. How sad I was for many days and weeks as I drove the hills and valleys of my practice and thought of my friend and his brave family. And often I thought of my own urge to take off my shirt in the middle of nowhere and work in the noonday sun, absorbing its friendly rays. I was grateful for my small decision to keep it on. His family is grown now, and I see some of his children from time to time at our clinic with their pets. We reminisce about days at the farm and their wonderful parents. Life goes on, and the results of their labors are seen daily in their children.

As I sat down to write this epistle, my friend Johnny One Eye jumped on my lap and then up on the computer, so I'm trying to type this while he rubs up against my chin with his tail and then headbutts me with his one-eyed face. He's a good friend and a courageous cat.

Sometimes veterinary medicine grosses even me out. I was on call today. This morning I saw several cases of varying conditions and etiologies. The most serious was a cat that came home this morning after being missing for three days. He had a good excuse. He was hit by a car several days ago, because his wounds were terrible, and they were infested with maggots, which took a few days to develop. The skin on his lower jaw was stripped from the bone and required sutures to be passed through the bone behind his lower incisors and through the skin of his dangling chin to be able to suture it back in place. He had two very deep gashes in his groin and over his back in the pelvic region. Both of these wounds were alive with fly larvae (maggots). It's a good thing I woke up today thinking it was fast Sunday. (On the first Sunday of every month, we fast for twenty-four hours and donate the money we would have spent on meals to the needy.) It was a job that needed to be done on an empty stomach. A splinter of bone from the pelvis needed to be removed before closing one of the wounds. Most of the time spent was used to remove the thousands of little helpers crawling around in there. The cat was, of course, under anesthesia the whole time and on IV fluids and pain medication and antibiotics. I just returned from checking on him at the clinic, and he was awake and recovering. Our night watchman will monitor him through the night along with several other patients there, including a seizuring dog I just admitted and placed on sedatives and IV fluids and insulin.

I was reminded again today of a scene I will spend the rest of my life trying to forget. When cows are out on pasture in the summer, they are exposed to the elements day and night. When a summer lightning storm comes up, they often group together under a tree. It was not uncommon to get a call the morning after a storm asking me to come out to a farm to autopsy a cow that was found dead for no apparent reason. The cows are usually insured against death by electrocution from lightning, but the insurance company requires a veterinary certification that lightning was the cause of death, which requires a veterinary autopsy. The wording of the veterinary report has to be cagey because if the case goes to court, one has to defend his/her diagnosis. So the statement should read something like "On such and such a date, I performed a necropsy on a cow owned by so and so. On the basis of my findings at that time, I cannot rule out lightning as the cause of death." If you say that the cause of death is lightning, then you have to show what you found that points to that diagnosis. If you word it right, you are just showing what the cow didn't die from and inability to rule out lightning as the cause. Much easier to defend in a court of law. Us vets can be cagey too.

One bright, sunshiny morning, I got the dreaded call to come check a cow that was found dead out in pasture. When I arrived at the farm, the farmer asked me to write up a lightning-strike statement as the cause of death. I indignantly stated that I needed to do an autopsy to confirm that as the cause of death before I could ever think of signing such a statement. So he shrugged his shoulders and told me to get my autopsy equipment out and get on his tractor so he could drive me out to where he found her. When we started across the pasture, I began to pick up the pungent, offensive odor of rotting flesh. As we got closer, the stench became oppressive. We stopped a hundred feet from the dead cow, which was bloated up three times her normal size and had a thick blanket of maggots surrounding her like the tide coming in at the beach. This cow had been dead a few days and was lying out in the hot summer sun. I realized that if I punctured the hide on that cow with my autopsy knife, we would all be blown to kingdom come, and in any case, I couldn't do an autopsy with one hand while the other covered my mouth and nose. I signed the statement and got the heck out of there. I think I can defend my action at the judgment seat.

My daughter Mallory and her husband, Garrett, have been working hard for us at the clinic and at our son Brent's boarding kennel all summer long. They are hard workers and excellent and compassionate in dealing with our clients. Today they left for their adventure to Grenada, where Garrett will be attending St. George University, school of veterinary medicine. They are taking their cat, Alfred, with them. Mallory researched the health chart and vaccination requirements on the Internet and by phone calls to the consulates and to the airline, and to the university to make sure we had every i dotted and every t crossed.

Their flight would leave at 12:50 AM (in about twenty minutes), and they arrived at the airport at noon so they would be there in plenty of time and with no stress. I filled out a health certificate for Alfred a week ago and updated all his vaccinations, did a physical, and made all the veterinary preparations required for the trip.

Upon checking into the airline at 11:00 PM, they were told that they needed a transit paper for the cat for their one-hour layover in Trinidad. Everyone she contacted before leaving said that the transit paper would not be necessary, and Trinidad's website said one was needed if arriving by boat and leaving by plane or if arriving by plane and leaving by boat, but no mention was made if arriving by plane and leaving by plane. So I talked by phone to an agent at the airline post at the airport who was about as sympathetic as a hooded executioner and who refused to give me the contact number of the Trinidad customs people who told him they couldn't come with the cat if they didn't have transit papers. I explained to him that I was a licensed veterinarian, accredited by the US Department of Agriculture, with the right to issue international health certificates, and would like to talk with the customs people who were refusing the cat, to which he basically replied *no*. So the choice they were given was to try to get the transit paper in the next few days and book another flight after that or go without the Alfred. What to do, what to do.

I hung up after talking to a very stressed daughter, who was on the verge of tears but nevertheless holding up well. I had to think about it for a minute. The wheels were grinding. It was too far to get there before their flight was to leave, get the cat, and bring him home, and no one at the airport would take him until I could get there, so the option of leaving without Alfred wasn't an option for tonight. This was like a difficult calving, and it was late at night as all difficult calvings were. *There is always a way, Dan, think. You can do this. But whatever you do, you have to do it now.*

After a few moments, I called Mallory back and asked her to check with a taxi stand to see if they would transport the cat back to Waterville by taxi and how much it would cost. She called back and said they would, but it would cost a thousand dollars. I did a quick calculation in my head and realized that if they all had to come back home and wait for transit papers and then travel back, it would cost more than that, not to mention that they had to make all their preparations once they got to Grenada before school started for Garrett. The plane was leaving in an hour. *What are you going to do, Dan?* So I had Mallory turn the cat over to the taxi driver after being reassured that they would take a credit card for payment since they would be arriving at 2:00 AM and I didn't have a thousand in cash on me. The taxi people were great, and I heard the relief and emotion in Mallory's voice when she called me back to tell me that Alfred was on his way home by taxi and they were going to make their flight. Now, reader, you know why I have such disdain for health certificates and officials who deal in such matters. I also added the Airlines to my list of disdainees, also Trinidad and flying in general. I'm going to bed, but I will soon be arising when Alfred arrives at 2:00-3:00 AM in his taxi. I must get a snack and a drink ready for him. If anyone reading this has a better solution than what I came up with, please keep it to yourself, or I will add you to my disdain list. On the upside, my daughter thinks I am a hero, so I'm happy.

This has been a great week. My older brother Mike visited with us all week, golfed with us, dined with us, mowed my grass, counseled with us, and blessed us with his wisdom and good spirit. At 4:30 AM, I arose and drove him to the airport in Syracuse and sent him on his way home to Arizona. I returned to work and my animal friends. I am on call all weekend, so whether or not I make it to church tomorrow is in the Lord's hands. I'll go where He wants me to go, be it to fellowship with my two-legged friends or to tend to His ailing four-legged friends. In either case, I will enjoy the day that is given to me and welcome whatever transpires.

I didn't make it to church today, but I found a way to make my own service of sorts. I went to the clinic to see some sick animals at 7:00 AM. I arrived at 6:30 AM and took care of the animals that were hospitalized for the weekend, feeding them, cleaning their litter boxes, and giving them their medications. I took care of continuing one cat on IV fluids and took blood from him to check his progress. It takes a great cat to be able to draw a blood sample without assistance and not leave the scene with any battle scars, but I succeeded. I left the clinic on foot for home at 9:15 AM, hoping to shower up and continue on for church at 10:00 AM in Utica. As I was walking down the highway to home, a neighbor called out to me and came over to meet me. She had a lot to tell me about cancer and diabetes in relatives and questions about how to take care of their dogs while they were in the hospital. I realized that today would not go as planned, but rather as directed, so I shifted gears to a slower speed and listened. I offered the clinic facilities to keep the dogs when Brent's kennels were full if she needed our help, and listened and occasionally gave moral support backed by the physical support of our clinic should the need arise. By the time I returned home, it was 10:00 AM, so I decided to forgo church since it would be almost over by the time I got there, and went instead to visit a couple of shut-in former clients I had, one housebound by a stroke and the other by age and arthritis. I had a good visit and left having given encouragement, fellowship, sympathy, and a gospel message, but I left more blessed than when I set out. I felt I was on the Lord's errand.

Later in the evening, I gave my daughter Mallory and her husband, Garrett, each a blessing. They would leave for Grenada tomorrow to begin Garrett's study of veterinary medicine and for Mallory to make her place among the people there. I blessed them both that they would be a great influence for good among their contacts there and that they would find wonderful opportunities for service leading to a great love for the people of that island. I have no doubt that by the time they leave the small branch of our church there, they will be sorely missed. So today was the type of Sabbath that was the norm for so many years before other veterinarians joined my practice and relieved me of my weekend duties. It was a good day.

I recall one day when I was practicing on my own, the phone rang one Sunday morning as I was preparing to leave for church. It was a client who raised heifers and who was a member of our church. Several of them, he said, were very sick with pneumonia, and the antibiotics he was treating them with weren't working. He didn't think they would survive until Monday. My heart sank as I realized that I was going to miss church once again. Then I had an inspirational thought. I told him to load all the sick calves in his trailer and bring them all to church. After sacrament meeting, I put on my rubber boots, and we worked our way through his trailer examining heifers, taking temperatures, and giving injections in the trachea and in the muscle and intravenously as the seriousness of the pneumonia warranted. I had my white shirt and tie on, but I rolled up my sleeves and tucked my suit pants into my boots. We were the best-dressed cattle handlers ever. I am sure when we went back to the rest of the meetings in the church, even though we looked good, our eau-de-corral scent wasn't as appealing, but we were so proud of ourselves for treating the sick calves and at the same time making it to church that we were oblivious to the obvious.

"And, behold, there was a man which had his hand withered. And they asked him, saying, Is it lawful to heal on the Sabbath days? That they might accuse him. And he said unto them, What man shall there be among you, that shall have one sheep, and if it fall into a pit on the Sabbath day, will he not lay hold on it, and lift it out? How much then is a man better than a sheep? Wherefore it is lawful to do well on the Sabbath days." Matthew 12:10

If I had one wish, I would wish to be able to do this: "Then saith he to the man, Stretch forth thine hand. And he stretched it forth; and it was restored whole, like as the other." Matthew 12:13

As it is, I will content myself in tending to my sick patients and lifting up the spirits of the downtrodden of my own species as best I can. I have seen joy and peace and comfort given to those who are troubled by a simple visit and a caring hand on the shoulder or a loving hug enough to know that this is how I wish to spend the rest of my days. I hope they are many.

Now that we have grandchildren of varying ages, a random flashback will come to me from time to time, of days long ago when our own children were toddlers and then mischief-makers. They would arise early in the morning and dress themselves hurriedly, hoping I would not have left yet on farm visits, knowing that if I hadn't had an emergency at 3:00 or 4:00 AM and left already, that they would be welcome riders with me for the day. One such day found me leaving at 5:30 AM for a calving. As I was pulling out of the bat cave (the heated garage under our bedroom where I kept my truck), two of them that hadn't started school yet came bursting out of the back door, pulling on their shirts and calling for me to wait. I stopped the truck, and they loaded up, and we were on our way. About midmorning, we arrived at a farm that had two boys the same age as mine for some routine work. My boys and they disappeared together while I went to work. As I was finishing up, one of my boys came into the barn in tears.

He had fallen into a pile of manure, and his pants were all dirty. So I looked at him and said, "OK, you're going to have to ride around for the rest of the day in your underwear," to which he replied in a pitiful cry, "I don't got no underpants!"

Fortunately, the mother at the farm was the one assisting me in the barn-cow duties. She laughed heartily and said don't worry, her boys were the same size, and she would lend him some clothes for the day. Thank you to all the compassionate mothers who were so understanding and helpful to this dad who wanted to be with his children so much but had little time, so he brought them with him to work.

They were always kind and understanding and willing to put up with their antics.

It takes a community to raise a child.

What a day! We had a busy schedule this morning, moving along smoothly with me in surgery and three other doctors doing appointments. Then all hell broke loose midmorning as a lady came in the door with a cat on a stretcher with a twenty-seven-inch arrow through his abdomen. It entered behind the rib cage, midway in the abdomen, almost perpendicular to his body, with twelve inches of arrow coming out one side with feathers attached to the end and twelve inches out the other side with the point of the arrow on that end. Someone shot this poor cat at close range and left him to wander around until he died, but that didn't happen. This Good Samaritan brought him to us as soon as she could. Everything came to a standstill at the clinic as two of the five veterinarians dropped everything, and several technicians joined in to tend to this cat. James admitted it and asked if he could follow up with surgery, which was just fine with me. Appointments backed up for a while as we focused on our new clinic cat, but we explained to our waiting clientele the reason for their wait, and everyone was understanding and indignant that someone would do this. We told the person who brought him in that we would cover the cost of everything for the cat if she would try to find a home for him, if he survived, to which she readily agreed.

The cat (we called him Norman) was put on an air heater because his body temperature was low. We started an IV. James cut the arrow on the feathered side, but we didn't pull it out yet. We drew blood to run to check for internal organ damage and blood counts to check for hemorrhage and infection as we prepared him for surgery. He was put on gas anesthesia and his abdomen shaved and prepared for surgery. James opened his abdomen and looked to see where the arrow passed and what the internal damage was. There was no hemorrhage, but it passed through the stomach. I pulled the arrow out slowly as James watched and pulled the stomach out of the abdomen as it was released from the arrow. There were four holes in it that started to leak ingesta into the abdomen as soon as the arrow came out. He exteriorized the stomach and held the holes shut as I sutured them one by one. The whole procedure took most of the rest of the morning to complete as his abdomen was washed with fluids several times and treated with antibiotics before closing him up, but the cat survived, and this evening, he was sitting up and doing fairly well. I would like to meet the primate that shot the arrow so I could suture his upper lip to his forehead and staple his head to the carpet. I took care of appointments with our other doctors until James finished with Norman, and then I went back to completing our regular surgeries.

I arrived home for lunch at one, having completed six hours of intensive veterinary medicine without an idle moment. My brain was going in high gear all morning, and when I got home, I flopped into a chair in mental and physical exhaustion. I rested a few minutes and then left to drive to Utica. I stopped halfway there on a country road and pulled over onto the shoulder, shut off the engine, and fell instantly asleep. I awoke twenty minutes later with a start, thinking I had gone off the road, until I came to enough to remember what had happened. I continued on about my afternoon's work: a visit to my elderly friend Jack to bring him some blueberry cookies Judy picked up at the Clinton farmers' market and a John Wayne T-shirt I picked up for him in Maine.

He gave me a small book entitled *The World According to Mister Rogers*, which has some wonderful observations about life. Then I left to travel to St. Luke's Hospital to visit an elderly couple who came to our clinic. They named their diabetic dog Danny after me. They both collapsed at home on Monday and were taken by ambulance to the hospital, and their neighbor brought in the dogs to us to take care of. I stopped to see how they were doing and to report to them that their dogs were happy. They were in adjoining rooms. The husband was delighted to see me and shook my hand several times. We visited awhile, and I don't think the president would have received a warmer welcome than I did. Then we went together to see his wife.

She was sleeping, but he gently woke her. She cried when she saw me standing by her bed and shook my hand. They were overjoyed to know that their dogs were doing well and that we had someone there twenty-four hours a day to watch them. We parted, each of us blessed by these few minutes together and all of us a little happier. It was one of those days when I rejoiced at my chosen career and was reminded that I dealt with people who happened to have animals. Thank you, Lord, for this blessed day.

Thankfully, I made it to the last hour of church this week. My heroes lie not in the football field, the basketball court, nor the cinema. My heroes are the men and women I meet with weekly at church who are my brothers and sisters and who live lives that are becoming the exception rather than the rule. There we meet to fellowship and strengthen one another for the week to come. Today I was feeling a little lonely and lost, going to church by myself as has become the norm in my life. We used to go with all our children and fill two whole pews, but now it's just Judy and I. My brothers and sisters smiled and shook my hand with enthusiasm as I entered and were sincerely glad to see me as was I to see them. They lifted my spirit and gave me renewed hope for the future.

As I stood in the lobby after church, waiting to meet with the ward clerk, I noticed an elderly sister sitting by herself with her walker, waiting for her ride home. She looked a little forlorn, so I walked over and shook her hand and asked her how things were going in her life. She said her trials seemed never ending. I had a choice then—to leave it at that and move on or to chat with her awhile. I knelt down on one knee by her side so I could talk to her face-to-face, and we visited for a few minutes. I asked her about some of the positive things that were going on in her life. I agreed with her that sometimes bad things seemed to snowball and try to crush us, but I pointed out the positive things in her life that she had just shared with me. I told her about Alfred, the thousand-dollar cat, and about Norman, the cat that we removed the arrow from his abdomen. Then her ride was leaving, and it was time to bid good-bye, but I think I may have helped her carry her load a little easier for a time by just taking the time to listen, sympathize, and encourage.

Thank you, Lord, for this busy day and the two hours that were given to me in the midst of it to go to your house of refuge and to be lifted up and to lift. For of such is the kingdom of God.

Chapter Nine

Home is Where the Heart is

Eight years ago, we built our new clinic on twenty-five acres, a mile outside of town. Judy asked if she could raise some chickens since it was in the country. So says Judy, so shall it be done. We put a chicken coup on the property and put in ten chickens and two roosters. They produced eggs for us, but mainly, they were just pets.

Especially Bob, the elder rooster. They were fascinating to watch. Bob took a liking to Judy and followed her everywhere like a puppy. As time went by, he developed a growth on his leg. I put him on antibiotics hoping it was an infection and not a tumor.

It continued to grow. Poor Bob followed Judy everywhere still, but more and more he struggled on one leg to keep up with her. The other chickens and especially the younger rooster sensed his disability and segregated and pecked him without mercy. We put him in a pen by himself when we saw what was going on. He still got very excited whenever Judy came out to visit him. Finally, I had to put him down. After working on large animals for so many years and considering myself to be a tough cowboy, I never in a million years thought that I would shed tears over a chicken. I was wrong. I loved Bob's spirit and his surprising devotion to my wife.

Peace

I had a farmer call me one July day in 1990 because his cow was up to her chest in mud and water in a drainage ditch. When I arrived, I followed his tractor with my truck to the scene. Sure enough, the cow was stuck down a six-foot steep embankment on either side of the ditch. There was no way that cow was coming out of there without me getting down and dirty. I had to get in there with her and pass ropes over her back and down her side then reach under her and pull them through to her other side, all the while watching in case she rolled over on me and drowned me. I made a harness this way, and then the farmer attached it to his tractor and dragged her out. I crawled out behind her, soaked in mud from head to toe. Those were fun days, but they were long and sometimes seemingly endless.

A few days ago, I went into one of our exam rooms for my next appointment.

There was a large dog (about German shepherd size) standing against the wall next to his owner. He looked at me with apprehension. I knelt down on the floor and began to talk to him. The owner said, "You might as well forget that—the last time, he needed a muzzle on and four people holding him down just to trim his nails."

I said, "Well, just give me a couple of minutes first." I knelt down so I was at his level. I talked quietly to him in peaceful tones. He slowly came over to me. I rubbed his ears and massaged them. I scratched his back, which he really loved.

Then I rubbed each of his front legs and then slowly raised each leg, one at a time. I spoke softly to him the whole time I was working on him. I clipped one toenail, then the rest. I moved slowly from foot to foot until all had been done, with no resistance from the dog. The owner's jaw was on the floor. He couldn't believe that we were able to do everything with no muzzle and minimal restraint. It just took patience—moving slowly with love and concern, step by step, to gain his confidence. Often my patients are very similar to their two-legged owners.

Home Sweet Home

Home to me is a great place. I can remember one night among thousands in particular when home was a welcome refuge. I worked all day in the cold of winter, attending to this cow and that calf, traveling many miles in between on treacherous roads. My last call of the day was to attend to a heifer, or young cow to you nonfarmers, delivering her first calf. By then it was dark, and she was down in the heifer barn and paralyzed in her hind end. I checked her over while the farmer held a flashlight. She was in a large open pen, which was almost knee-deep in muck. As I checked her, my heart sank as I realized that the only way we were going to get that calf out was by C-section. I was cold and wet from my day's work and dog tired. The wind was whipping through the barn, and it was a filthy place to do surgery, not to mention the lack of light. So my home not being two miles away, I told the farmer I'd be back in half an hour to do the task. I think that night, I felt the most despair at my chosen career that I had ever felt. I drove home and took a long hot shower to drive the cold from my bones. Then I put on some clean, dry clothes and a turtleneck shirt. I drove back to the farm with great apprehension and found to my delight that the farmer had cleaned away the muck from around the heifer, brought in a trouble light, closed the barn door, and had a salamander heater blowing warmth all around her and fresh straw spread around her for me to kneel on. The whole evening, as I completed the task before me, was made bearable by my thoughts of home and family. Bright in my mind was the picture of our woodstove merrily pouring out lovely penetrating heat and my wife and children awaiting my return. Home to me is a place where I can come after such a day and feel the cares of the day and of the world fall away.

My children mostly grew up on the road with me traveling from farm to farm from early morning until late at night. I told my wife that once they were housebroken, I would take them with me on farm calls. I did not want to be changing diapers in the dead of winter on some side road. Consequently, from about the age of three until they began kindergarten, they would be up at the crack of dawn, dressed and with their boots on, eager to join me on the roads and to witness the multitude of wonders that were ours to witness as we tended to God's four-legged creatures in four counties of New York State. Often I would carry them in asleep from my truck late into the evening and put them carefully into their beds. They traveled with me every day from farm to farm, administering to the health needs of cows, horses, goats, sheep, pigs, and all manner of other creatures. They had certain jobs that they performed when we arrived. When we dehorned cattle, they gathered the horns and put them in a plastic bag. They told the farmer they were taking the horns home so their mother could make horn soup. When we arrived at a farm, they would run a pail of hot water for me in the milk house while I began examining the animals. If I needed any medication or tools, they would go back to my truck to get them. One of their favorite jobs was delivering calves. While I began sorting out arms and legs and a head in preparation for the delivery, they would choose a clean straw or strand of hay. When the calf was delivered, it would lie motionless on the ground, exhausted from the delivery. Then they would quickly tickle its nose with the straw to make it sneeze. Once the calf sneezed, it would clear the fluid from its chest and take a deep breath, and then we knew that it would be all right and begin to awaken to the new world we just introduced it to. It gave my children a great sense of importance and purpose to be able to be instrumental in stimulating those newborn calves to come alive before their very eyes.

We usually left early in the morning to go to the first farm. After we completed each visit, we would call the office to find out where all the sick animals were and plan our day. As the number of calls piled up, we would sometimes become discouraged and wonder how we would ever get done as we looked at the long list of farms we had to visit. Then we would roll up our sleeves and head out down country roads to begin our tasks at hand. As we drove, we sang a favorite pioneer song. All is well.

After they began school, we would look forward to the weekends when they could once again join me on our adventures. As they grew older, I began to feel like Puff the magic dragon when little Jackie came no more. But as they approached the end of their high school career, they worked more and more with me, looking to earn some funds for college. Finally, our eldest son received a mission call for far-off Norway to serve a period of two years, during which time we would not see him.

The night before he left, I went into his room for the last time, at about 1:00 AM. I watched him sleeping and realized that this would be the last time I would be checking on him for two years. As I tucked him in, I wondered, as I listened to his breathing, if I had gone fishing with him enough or played ball with him enough.

Did I teach him everything he would need to know about life to make it through the next two years? Did I do enough with him in scouts, and was I there for him when he needed me? A lump swelled in my throat, and I shed a quiet tear or two.

There was so much more I would like to have done with him, but our time was up for now, and it was time for him to go. The words of the song after which I was named came to mind: "O Danny Boy, the pipes the pipes are calling, from glen to glen and down the mountain side. The summer's gone and all the flowers are dying, 'tis you, 'tis you must go and I must bide. But come ye back when summer's in the meadow, or when the valley's hushed and white with snow, 'tis I'll be here in sunshine or in shadow, O Danny Boy O Danny Boy, I love you so."

I have learned in my life that nothing is easy. There are a few people who win the lottery and are "blessed" with an instant fortune. I'm not one of them. There are people who learn things in school very easily and do very well on tests. I'm not one of them. There are people whose education has been completely paid for by scholarships and/or family. I'm not one of them. I have had to work hard for everything I have been able to accomplish. I attend the school of hard knocks, which has the most expensive tuition, but you never forget the lessons. When I began veterinary college, my father sent me off with this one piece of advice:

> The heights by great men reached and kept, were not attained by sudden flight. But they while their companions slept, were toiling upward through the night. *Henry Wadsworth Longfellow*

I have recited this to myself countless times as I headed out into the night on a calving or some other emergency. It is a great privilege we have of being able to work and progress and learn from our mistakes and rejoice in our successes. I am thankful to my Father in heaven for the privilege I have of being a member of this living school we all attend. Do not be discouraged; God is over all.

When I was attending veterinary college, I worked on a dairy farm in Fergus, Ontario, on weekends and summers to support our family, to gain some farm experience with large animals, and to become acquainted with the things farmers have to deal with on a daily basis. The lady who hired me was in her seventies. Her husband died from injuries sustained in a car accident some ten years earlier, and she was determined to keep the family farm in operation. She milked the cows morning and night, 7 days a week, 365 days a year. She was a former schoolteacher. She had phlebitis in her legs, and she was stooped over from arthritis, but she had the spirit and drive of a young woman. She was an inspiration to me and taught me many invaluable things in the four years that I worked for her. After morning chores, we (the hired men and women) would go out to do fieldwork, such as planting, haying, woodcutting, fencing, etc., while she would busy herself preparing dinner for all of us. She would set the table saying, "Bread and butter, milk and sugar, salt and pepper." She would always prepare a large lunch and supper consisting of roast beef, potatoes, vegetables, and a wonderful dessert. At the conclusion of the meal, we would all visit a little, discussing the morning's work and preparing for the afternoon's labor, then everyone would leave the table and go back to work in the fields. No one would say anything about the meal nor compliment or thank this hardworking gentlewoman. I took it upon myself to daily tell her what a great meal it was and to inquire of its ingredients. I got the recipe from her for poor man's pudding and learned that if you boil potatoes with onions, the onions won't flavor the potatoes, and they will have a much milder taste after boiling and be delicious with butter. A few simple words of gratitude and recognition of her labors were all that were needed for us to become lifelong friends.

Inch by Inch

A few months ago, we operated on a dog that had swallowed half a tube of Gorilla Glue. When it hits the stomach, it expands and hardens. She had been vomiting all day. When she came in, I felt her abdomen and could feel a very large hard mass, so we took her right into surgery. We removed a volleyball-sized firm mass from her stomach that bounced like a ball when I dropped it on the floor. Her incision was sixteen inches long, and for two days she was a sorry-looking dog, but she is now bouncing off the wall again. If you have animals, please hide the Gorilla Glue.

I remember one day a long time ago when my son Brent and I left early in the morning to a calving that ended up being a horrible caesarean on a cow that had dead twins—they had been dead for over a week, so it was pretty bad. We finished suturing her up and went back to the truck to call in and get the calls for the day. I listened to the list of calls and began writing them down. Brent watched beside me as the list grew longer and longer. At first, we both despaired of ever getting home, but as the list lengthened, we both began to smile as we realized the hopelessness of ever getting done and resigned ourselves to trying. In the end, we had twenty-three farm calls that day and traveled over three hundred miles to complete them. The last call of the day was as the first call of the day—a caesarean on a cow—but we finally finished up and arrived back home after midnight, having left that morning before 5:00 AM. Brent was very stoic that day, never complaining, making good conversation, and we helped each other keep our sanity.

I have learned in life that when faced with an insurmountable task, to put my head down, plow ahead, and take each task one at a time, and in the end, the job will be done. I am very grateful for the road that life has taken me down and very grateful for my family that has loyally traveled much the same road with me. We have our disagreements from time to time, but we are fiercely loyal to one another and have been through so much together. I feel very sad for the mistakes that have been made, but I am looking to the future and redemption.

Chapter Ten

Winter Sabbath

Fall has arrived with its beautiful colors, the smell of freshly fallen leaves, the life-renewing rain, the cooler weather, and the promise of winter. It is a time for the earth to rest from all its labors and to renew itself. For a large-animal practitioner, it is a pleasant time when the weather is more conducive to hard labor and the insects have all but disappeared. I love the fall, but the winter is another subject.

At first it is beautiful and enjoyable, with its white blanket and the smell of firewood burning brightly in the stove, but later it becomes tedious and requires long-suffering. As I write this, a small nine-week-old kitten lies on my lap, tired from his day's activities and content to enjoy the warmth and security of my lap. We named him Cochise, but my daughter who lives in Virginia heard Goat Cheese over the phone. I think her name is the one that will stick. No respect for the Old West, these youngsters. We have another kitten we just adopted. He was brought to the clinic with one eye swollen twice the normal size and infected. I had to remove it surgically, and then we kept him for a day after the surgery, and then another day and another, finally realizing that the owner was not coming back. We named him Johnny One Eye. He bounces all over the place chasing Goat Cheese and our older cat, Unca Rico. He cares not that he only has one eye or that someone chose to desert him. He faces each day with joy and wonder. He finds fascination in a paper bag. He relishes each meal. He loves everyone, and every day is more exciting than the last. His love is unconditional. Couldn't we all take a lesson from him? Wait, Johnny One Eye, that's my cold meat slice you are making off with!

I love it when I get a second chance. I remember one early morning in Vermont when I was called to treat a cow that was comatose with milk fever (hypocalcemia). Her blood pressure was dangerously low, and she was close to death. This called for immediate administration of an IV solution of calcium. I tried twice to get a needle into the jugular vein and failed. Before I wound up for the third try, the farmer quietly said, "Three strikes and you're out, Doc." I smiled when I looked at him, but I could see by the tone of his eyes that he was serious.

Fortunately, I succeeded on my third attempt, and we saved the cow from certain death.

I entered an exam room at our clinic a few weeks ago to check a dog. The owner sat on a chair with a headpiece on to a telephone. He was seemingly talking into midair. As I entered, he said, "OK, I love you." I replied with a sheepish grin, "I love you too, man." That drew a strange look—no sense of humor. He had a young son with him. After checking their puppy, I noticed how close the son was to his dog. I asked the little boy his name, to which he replied, "Duncan." I thought that was a pretty British-sounding name for central New York, so I asked his father how he happened to pick that name, to which he replied that he met the boy's mother coming out of Dunkin Donuts.

One frigid morning, I traveled to a farm in the hills of central New York to check a cow that was having a difficult time delivering her calf. She was in a large pen that was freshly bedded with straw. We haltered her and tied her up to the fence.

I washed her up and put my arm in to see what was holding things up. The calf was huge! There was no sense trying to deliver this calf any other way than by C-section. I got some pails of hot water while the farmer ran an electrical cord to the pen. I clipped the whole side of the cow, washed and scrubbed her, then injected several syringes full of lidocaine, a local anesthetic, along the impending incision line, which would end up being about thirty inches long, just behind the rib cage. By the time I started the surgery, my wet hands were beginning to get frostbite. The surgery was done while the cow was standing. She never fussed or tried to escape, which told me my nerve block was successful. I used all my strength and had my arm up to my neck into her abdomen to exteriorize part of the uterus with a hoof inside. I incised the uterine wall and grasped the hoof inside, then found the other hoof and pulled the calf out through the abdominal wall. It took everything I and the farmer had to pull that calf out, holding on to the uterus after the calf was delivered so it could be sutured and safely closed. It was the largest calf I had ever delivered, and it was very weak. The farmer worked on reviving the calf while I sutured up the cow. By the time I was all done, the cow, the calf, and I were all shivering from hypothermia. I left and went on to the rest of my duties for the day. I returned the next morning to check on the cow.

The farmer was not there, for which I was grateful, half expecting to find a dead calf and a dying cow in the barn when I looked in. I reluctantly entered the barn to find the cow in her pen, chewing her cud contentedly with her calf vigorously nursing at her side. I don't know if it was fatigue from the previous day's work or relief that both were doing well, but I was greatly moved as I stood there for a few minutes watching them and rejoiced that my efforts had not been in vain. A mother and her child is an inspiring sight, no matter what the species.

As I have gained experience in veterinary medicine, I have learned to choose carefully what I say to clients. I pulled in to a farm one morning whistling a tune and feeling pretty good about the world. Most of my farm clients were cheerful, hardworking people who enjoyed the work they were engaged in. This particular farmer was not. He was pretty grumpy. I learned to choose my words carefully when speaking with him. As I walked into the barn, I spotted him and greeted him with a cheerful "Mornin'," to which he immediately replied, "What's good about it?" and then went on to berate me for even thinking it was a good morning and how dare I say good morning considering all the things he was up against at the start of the day. I let him unload and then I said, "I didn't say *good* morning, I just said morning." He smiled a little, and we began our work.

Late one evening, a beagle came into the clinic with a mangled tail, run over by a car. That was all that was wrong with him, but it was enough. I could not repair it, so I removed it. He went home happy the next day, and the owners were thankful that I took them in late at night and tended to their beloved pet. But one day later, they called to say he had chewed out his stitches and needed to be resutured. They were angry that I hadn't warned them about this possibility nor sent them home with a collar to prevent him from doing so. Their neighbor called me up and called me every name in the book. I resutured the dog and sent them home with an e-collar, but I felt sorrow that in their indignation, they saw no fault in their own shepherd's responsibility but most of all that they and their neighbor negated twenty-three years of rising up in the middle of the night whenever the phone rang to roll out in the cold dead of night, to drive many miles on treacherous roads, to tend to God's creatures in their hour of need. They made their judgment of me based on one isolated incident.

I stood in line at a hardware store one afternoon, not for hardware but to order a delicious sausage and onions, the aroma of which drew me from my intended route to the store for hardware to a much higher mission. As I stood there, an elderly gentleman and his wife were walking carefully and slowly into the sore, age and arthritis having taken their toll on their bodies. A young man brisked by them, exclaiming all kinds of obscenities to them as he rushed into the store. I was caught by surprise and didn't know what to make of what I had seen and heard, but as I stood there waiting and thinking, I surmised that he must have had to wait behind them in his car as they drove slowly into the parking lot, or perhaps, they may have inadvertently cut him off in turning into the parking lot. I thought, you know, my father fought as a pilot in World War II, raised a family, and lived an honorable life of service to his fellowman, and perhaps, this elderly man who was the target of your abuse landed on the beaches of Normandy. In another time, he might have laid you flat in the parking lot for using such language around his sweetheart. We owe the elderly the room and respect they earned.

As I visit the sick in the hospitals and in the nursing homes, I am haunted by the faces of the people I pass in the hallways that look at me as though to say, "Are you here to see me? Won't you stop to visit with me or just to say hello?" I visited a lady in a nursing home here in Utica that I used to have as a client. She always had beagles. They were her great love. She worked tirelessly caring for housebound seniors to pay for the care of her beloved dogs, never complaining. I loved to have her come to the clinic. She was always cheerful and glad to see us.

One day, she became one of the patients for whom she had cared. She was very surprised to see me and excited to have the company. I realized in our visit how much she missed her dogs. I returned to visit her again one Sunday evening. She wasn't in her apartment. As I returned to the desk to ask her whereabouts, an elderly lady in a wheelchair in the hall shouted to me, "Doctor, she's in the hospital wing in room 213. She'll be so happy you came to see her." My heart was touched that her friend was excited for her that someone had come to see her. I realized that she would never leave the assisted care facility again and her daughters had taken in or found homes for the beagles.

I went to a stuffed teddy bear store in Syracuse one Saturday and found a beagle to stuff. I placed a heart in it, named it, got a birth certificate for it, and had it stuffed and sutured up. The next week, I delivered it to my friend in the hospital. I think she was as excited to receive that beagle as any of her other ones from the past. I went to visit her on several occasions after that. The last visit, she was in the hospital again but excited that her pneumonia was getting better and that they would be returning her to her apartment soon. Three days later, I sat down at my desk to check my messages and make a few phone calls. There, on a sticky note, was a message from her daughter saying that she had passed away. That note hit me as hard as any cow had ever kicked me. I sat there and couldn't speak. I gathered myself together in a few minutes and went back to work. I called her daughter the next day to find out about her, but I found myself unable to speak, so I just asked if she had a picture of her mother, and would she bring it by the clinic so I could place it on the wall in our waiting room in her honor, which is where it is to this day.

My friend and I visited an elderly man we know from church, in another nursing home just before Christmas. He seemed so lonely. I went to the store the next day and picked up some Christmas decorations, and we returned a few days later and decorated his room. For days after we left, the nurses and many of the residents crowded into his room to see the Chipmunks sing their Christmas song on a small stage we left as part of the decor. Our family, including my friend, went to the home just before Christmas. He was eating in the cafeteria with his roommates.

We gathered around his table and sang Christmas carols to him. All the residents stopped eating and focused on us. They applauded when we were done.

One of the men at his table looked at us with tears in his eyes and thanked us for thinking of his friend and for coming to brighten their day. It was our privilege.

I have another friend we visited one Sunday, my family and I. He is a veteran of World War II and used to bring his dog to our clinic for medical attention. In the last few years, he became too feeble to leave his house, so I traveled there from time to time to check on his dog but mainly to check on my friend and offer companionship. After visiting with him over the years, I discovered that he played the harmonica. We went to his home on Christmas Eve to sing some carols for him. We learned that his harmonica was broken, so Mallory, Judy, and I went to the music store a couple of days later and purchased a new one, which we delivered to him a few days later. He played us such a concert. Normally, he had a very difficult time walking, but for a short time, his legs danced a jig and stomped time to the music as though fifty years had disappeared. His face brightened with a smile of his youth. We had a wonderful time with my friend. I continue to phone him and visit from time to time to check on him, listen to war stories, and enjoy his harmonica.

As Judy and I were leaving Utica on vacation some time ago, en route to Nova Scotia to visit relatives, we stopped by another nursing home to visit a ninety-six-year-old client who brought his dog Georgie to our clinic for so many years. His wife and daughter continued to care for Georgie, but my friend was now confined to the home. I had just recently learned from his wife and daughter on their latest visit with Georgie that he was now residing there, so I determined to visit my loyal friend. As I walked into his room, his face filled with amazement, and his eyes twinkled. He looked at me as though I were the president of the United States. He exclaimed, "I can't believe you came to see me here." I was humbled and gratified by his greeting and came to the realization that this visit meant so much to him and cost me only a few short moments of my time. We visited for a time, and I listened with sadness to his realization that this place was now home for him, and he could only receive his longtime bride of seventy years as a visitor. We cried a little, and we laughed a little, and I tried to encourage him as we reminisced about our experiences together as veterinarian-client. Finally, I stood to leave explaining that my wife was waiting in the parking lot and we needed to begin our long drive to Nova Scotia. I grasped his hand as I left for a final handshake as tears filled his eyes. He asked if I would kiss him good-bye. I leaned over this humble man sitting in his wheelchair and hugged him and kissed him on the cheek and asked God to bless him. I felt at that moment, as I had before on rare occasions, that I stood on holy ground. I promised to return to visit, which I did regularly until he passed the way of all living things. Life is sometimes sad and sometimes joyful, but I wouldn't trade it for anything. In the words of Alfred, Lord Tennyson, "It is better to have loved and lost than never to have loved at all."

The other day, I went into the local quick stop to buy lunch. As I was waiting, I looked to my right and saw an old friend standing and smiling at me. It was a farmer for whom I worked for many years as his veterinarian. As a matter of fact, he was one of the first to call me to his farm when I was a new veterinarian in the area some twenty-three years ago. He was one of the brave who was willing to take a chance to see what this new young vet could do for his cows, which, incidentally, were his livelihood. I hadn't seen him in quite a while since I had moved and had given up large-animal work seven years ago. At one time I saw him weekly, sometimes daily, often nightly. He broke into a broad grin and put out his hand. He was a sight for sore eyes, and after all that we had been through over the years, working together in the wee hours of the morning to save his animals, in the cold of winter or heat of summer, a handshake just didn't seem enough, so I threw my arms around him and gave him a big Canadian hug. There is a friendship that comes from working together through adversity. I appreciate these longtime friends of mine who work so hard.

We had dinner with another farm client and his wife this summer, not having seen them for a while. A flood of old memories comes over me when reunited with these comrades. I'm beginning to feel older and more emotional than I used to. I even enjoy shopping and watching the food channel. I am thankful to my Maker for the wonderful associations I have made in my work over the years. Although I am working on small animals now, in my heart I still think of myself as a farm veterinarian and feel honored that these fine gentlemen number me as one of them.

This spring, we bade a sad farewell to our old friend Jesse. Jesse was our family dog for the past twelve years. We adopted him when he was two years old. Our children grew up with him. He was Judy's faithful friend for so many years while I was away for extended times, taking care of a growing practice and being bishop at our church. He was always excited and overjoyed to see Judy come home. He sat faithfully and quietly at her feet all day long and slept between us on our bed. He never had a sick day in his life, and when he finally did, I couldn't save him. When he became sick, we took him into surgery but discovered a bleeding aneurysm in his abdomen that we couldn't stop. While he was still under anesthesia, I released him from his ailing body. There was much sadness around our clinic that day. Each of us choked back tears for many days as we thought of our faithful friend and all the memories of his kind and joyful demeanor. I was very proud of our family through it all, though, as we honored his memory with a quiet and respectful sadness and carried on in our duties in the animal kingdom.

As he lay lifeless on the surgery table, I disconnected all the equipment and IVs and wrapped him gently in a blanket. I bent over him on the table and gave him a final hug and shed some tears for our faithful friend and member of our family.

They really don't live long enough and we become too attached, but Jesse will always be with us in our hearts and minds.

It's 10:00 PM and I'm at the clinic, checking on things and starting an IV on a small dog that came in tonight in kidney failure. I love to be here at the clinic in the late evening when everything is quiet. The animals are all settled down for the night, the phone isn't ringing, and the waiting room is empty. Such a contrast from the daytime. We are blessed with work, but the peace and quiet come over me like a wave. That's one of the things I miss in large-animal work—the quiet refuge of my beloved truck in between farm visits. However, there is much danger out there on the road.

One winter morning, there was a film of ice on all the roads, enough to close the schools for the day. Weather doesn't stop a large-animal veterinarian though. We thrive on danger. Brent decided he would travel with me that morning as he did whenever he had a day off school. We set out up the King Settlement Road, a winding trail, going over hill and valley and around many a turn. We came up over the crest of a hill, on a road of sheer ice, traveling about 25 mph. Ahead of us was a huge milk truck, stopped in the middle of the highway, unable to travel farther due to ice. Coming down the road in the opposite lane was another pickup, blocking me from passing. I stepped on the brakes, the wheels locked, but my truck just kept sliding full speed ahead toward the back end of a truck full of milk. I told Brent to hold on, we had no place to go, so get ready for a collision. Just at the last second, I spotted a ramp built over the deep ditch on the right side to allow tractors and hay wagons access to the field.

I swerved toward the ditch, down the ramp, into the hayfield and a foot of snow, just a few feet before the milk truck. We slid halfway across the field and came to rest near the fence on the opposite side. I figured we'd be stuck there for the rest of the day but breathed a sigh of relief that we were alive and intact. I put the truck in four-wheel drive, and to my joy, we walked right out of that field of snow like it was the middle of summer. Thanks to the powers that be for four-wheel drive. I learned a lesson that day. Never give up hope. No matter how hopeless the situation, always be vigilant, ever watching for the opportunity to turn things around, even up to the last second before impending disaster. Also, stay off the road when it's icy. I know there was more than Brent and me in the truck that day and on many, many others.

On a very busy night a few months ago, I walked past a waiting room full of people and their pets into the exam room to do a routine checkup and vaccination of a golden retriever. I thought it would be a quick visit and then on to the next appointment. As I visited with the owner, I realized that he needed more from me than just a physical for his dog. In the course of the visit, he shared with me his own story. He completed three tours of duty in Vietnam as a ground crew chief for the air force. On his last tour, he was critically injured as a mortar shell exploded near him, causing internal injuries that kept him in the hospital for several months. As he and his wife approached retirement a couple of years ago, they purchased an RV and adopted a dog and made preparations to travel the country. Six months before his childhood sweetheart was to retire, she became ill and passed away within a few weeks. I put his file aside and spent some time just listening to him. I call him every couple of weeks to check up on him and just visit.

Last Saturday, I took him out to breakfast. Sometimes my work requires less time with the animal and more time with the owner. Maybe the best gift of all is the gift of our time and a listening ear.

Coz was a one-hundred-pound husky, German shepherd dog that lived close to our veterinary clinic. He was a large shy dog who wasn't very popular in our neighborhood. He took delight in beating up the dogs of the neighbors as they passed by on walks and in terrorizing our clients and their animals as they came to our clinic. Garbage day for Coz was a spiritual experience as he roamed the area sampling from the smorgasbord of delicacies hidden behind green plastic and spreading his meal all over the street and lawns. He beat up our family dog when we moved into the neighborhood. When his owner needed to bring him to the clinic for a checkup or a haircut or when he became ill, she had to call her son from across town to drag and carry him into our dreaded clinic.

One stormy night at about 8:00 PM, I was preparing to leave for home. Lightning was snapping all around us. As I turned out the lights and shut down the clinic after a busy day, I opened the front door, and in walked Coz, his tail between his legs, terrified of the lightning. He cowered over in the corner of the waiting room behind a chair. My first impulse was to throw him out the door and rejoice that his just deserts were finally coming to him. But compassion tweaked my heart as I looked at that pathetic sight. My dinner would already be cold anyway. I closed the door and went to the desk to do some paperwork for a few minutes and wait with Coz for the storm to pass. When the tempest outside passed, I opened the door, and Coz filed out, heading for home, and I followed. We both learned something that night. Coz learned that I was his friend, and I learned that he was only human.

A voice from the past.

A few months ago, while I was visiting my mother in Ottawa, she reminded me that a friend of hers from the past, whose daughters I went to high school with, was living in an assisted-living apartment in Niagara Falls. It brought to memory my last encounter with her some five years previous. She was a stalwart member of our church. She worked tirelessly with her husband in our little branch in Ottawa.

They and my parents and many other members worked on numerous fund-raisers to finally acquire the funds to begin construction on a new church building. We were all one big family back then. I picked up their daughters each morning at five thirty to go to early morning scripture study class at our new church building and then dropped them off at school afterward. They were like sisters to me. We grew up together. At a reunion six years ago of all the old members of the Ottawa church, the girls' mother, on seeing me for the first time in twenty-five years, strode over to me with a mischievous grin and said, "Danny Gilchrist. I remember when our daughter began high school. You were a senior at her school. She was so shy and nervous about going to high school for the first time. We finally coaxed her into going.

"She felt lost in the hallway between classes on the first morning with hundreds of students going from one class to the next. Then she saw a familiar face down the hall. It was you. She ran up to you and exclaimed, 'Danny, it's so good to see you.' You looked at her and spoke in a loud voice for all to hear, 'KISS YOU—I HARDLY EVEN KNOW YOU.' She was mortified."

After all these years, she was laughing as she related this story, but as a father of two daughters, I understand that at the time, I'm sure she would have cheerfully wrung my neck. For the last five years, I thought once in a while of my thoughtless act and how it might have affected this young girl. When my mother told me of her old friend's whereabouts and that her daughter would be visiting her there at different times, I was determined to make the four-hour drive to Niagara Falls at a time when she would be there to visit with both of them and to apologize to her in front of her mother for my thoughtless act some forty years earlier. It was a joyful reunion, and I was glad I made the journey to see them. They said they had laughed many times over that incident. She freely forgave me, for which I will always be grateful. When I stood to leave, her mother asked me for a hug. I leaned over to accommodate her, and she said in a firm voice, "I want a real hug." I helped her stand from her wheelchair and hugged her. It was a happy ending to a very long story.

The following story is dedicated to my niece and her sister and sister-in-law; my wife, Judy, and daughter Erin; my own mother; and all good mothers wherever you may be.

Being a large-animal veterinarian is tiring, but being a mother is exhausting. My hat is off to all of you, but do not despair. Someday a brave soldier or budding violinist or conscientious plumber or compassionate teacher or tired veterinarian will say, "I had been taught by my mother that if I did not doubt, God would deliver [help] me."

Sleep has always been a necessary evil for me. My duties covering emergencies often kept me out on the road until late in the evening, then I would stay up later working on projects or the books or relaxing a little before checking in. I was too stubborn to go to bed early but too busy to sleep in past early dawn. It made for a dangerous combination when I was driving to farms. Fortunately, the farms usually weren't more than fifteen or twenty minutes apart, which didn't give me a lot of time to doze off. Nevertheless, I was in danger.

One day in the late fall, I left home before dawn on an emergency and then continued on through the day going from one farm to the next, tending to sick animals, doing routine visits, and taking care of emergencies in between. There was a steady stream of calls all day, into the evening and through the night, and starting up again the next morning. My first visit of the second day was to a cow that had just had a calf and couldn't get up.

She had milk fever or hypocalcemia, which resulted from the sudden call for calcium in her flush of milk, causing her muscles to weaken from the drop in calcium. The treatment is usually simple: two pints of 23 percent calcium given slowly in the jugular vein.

I warmed up two bottles of calcium in my five-gallon pail, inserted my needle into the cow's jugular vein, and began the calcium. I sat down on my pail and rested my elbow on my knee, so my arm was at the square holding the bottle up a few inches above the cow's head, allowing the calcium to drip into her vein by gravity. I blinked. Then I blinked more slowly. Then I fell asleep, sitting on my pail at the cow's side. When I opened my eyes, I looked at the empty bottle in my hand. I looked at the cow, who was much brighter and ready to arise. Then I looked ahead to the farmer, who was standing there grinning. I hoped he hadn't noticed that I had dozed off and flushed with embarrassment when he said, with a certain amount of sympathy in his voice, "Have a rough night, Doc?"

I worked all that day, stopping for a ten-minute nap by the roadside a couple of times. My last call came at midnight for a calving. I had been on the road for forty-one hours. By now I was running on adrenaline. I was interested by then to see how much I could accomplish. It had bypassed delirium, and now it was a challenge. I finally returned home at 2:00 AM. I was totally exhausted. I drove to within one block of home and could not go another inch. I pulled over to the side of the road, perpendicular to the curb, shut off the truck, and instantly fell asleep. I returned to consciousness when I heard a tapping at my window. I rolled the window down. It was a state trooper, checking to see if I was alive. He put his head almost into my truck, I suppose checking to see if he could smell alcohol. Having worked on cows for the last forty-one hours, he probably wished he had smelled alcohol. He asked in a quiet voice if I was all right. I explained to him that I was just returning from a calving and was pretty tired. Being in a rural area, he understood what was going on. "OK, Doc, start up the truck, and I'll follow you home to make sure you get there all right." I obeyed, drove three hundred yards, and pulled into my driveway. He stopped at the roadside, looked at me, scratched his head, and drove off. Exhaustion does some strange things to people.

I arose early the next morning. It was Sunday, but I had a couple of sick cows to check on, then I returned home, showered up, and went to church. I had a class of young people to teach. Somewhere in my schedule that week, I prepared a lesson for them. One thing about large-animal work is that one has a lot of time to think and develop ideas, traveling from farm to farm. There was a particularly touching story I wanted to read to my students. As we sat in a circle in the classroom, I opened the lesson book and began reading the story. I fell asleep midsentence. I don't know how long I was out, but when I opened my eyes, all the chairs were empty, and I sat alone in the classroom. When I realized what had happened, I opened the door to the class and looked into the laughing faces of my students, all standing in the hallway. A prophet hath no honor in his own home. I laughed right along with them.

I am not used to working for a living. Being back on the job for three weeks now finds me feeling very tired but also at peace. Morning begins at 5:00 AM as I rise up and begin the day. Judy, Murphy, and I leave home at around six every morning to ride to the bank, McDonald's in Clinton, and to drive through the country meadows that used to be my office. It's good to watch the sun come up while driving down a country road. I have always loved the early morning, and even when not working or on vacation, I'm up early to greet the day. We went for so many years without a day off that I hate to waste a single minute of time sleeping. Sleep to me is a necessary evil. Unfortunately, it has become my constant companion. Yesterday in the midst of a busy afternoon, a longtime client and her small dog came in for their usual checkup. Eight years ago, she used to come in with her husband, who was always well dressed. He was a short man, about the same height as his wife, neatly groomed, wearing a crisp white shirt and conservative tie and business suit.

He was always well-mannered and friendly and respectful, and I liked him and admired this couple. They are about my age. Seven years ago, he had a stroke, a severely disabling one, which ended our annual visits and sick ones in between.

Each year since, his wife has come in alone with their dog. I always ask about her husband, and she says he is doing OK but unable to walk very well and stays at home all the time. He was forced to retire from his work.

Each year I have had it in my mind after our visit to call on him. I always failed to follow through on that prompting. The Lord has been kind to me in my lifetime and given me many chances to redeem myself, for which I will always be grateful. This year, after our visit, I made a firm resolve that I would visit my old client. I asked about him, half expecting to hear he had passed away, but rejoiced that he was still with us. Last night, I printed up the first chapter of my book from my computer, and this afternoon, I stopped at their house. Their dog greeted me with her bark as I rang the doorbell, and she never stopped barking the whole time I was there. She sat in the living room eight feet from me and barked until I stood to leave. I admire her stubbornness and her refusal to compromise her standards. I think she remembered the injections I gave her at the clinic yesterday. It's OK, though; I still love dogs. His wife took me into their living room to stand by his chair. He is paralyzed on his right side and sits in a wheelchair with his legs raised up like a recliner. He smiled a crooked smile when I walked in and sat at his side. We visited for a time and caught up on some of the events in our lives over the last seven years since last we met. I gave him the copy of part of my book, which his wife will read to him. As I stood to leave, he rolled on his side so he could extend his left hand to shake mine.

His wife followed me to the door and thanked me for coming with a tender smile.

I know I brought some relief from the mundane into their lives this afternoon, and I promised to return in a week or so to get their critique of my stories. They need a friend, and I want the job. Thank you, Lord, for being patient with me.

Atrial fibrillation is a condition of the upper chambers of the heart, which will, for one reason or another, stop contracting in a regular rhythm and begin spastic, uncoordinated contractions. The ventricles or lower chambers of the heart normally take their cue for a contraction from a contraction of the upper chamber.

When atrial fibrillation occurs, the lower chambers take up a rhythm of their own, but that is interrupted every two or three beats by an electrical stimulus from the upper chambers, which occurs sporadically with this condition. It results in an irregular heartbeat. I have had this condition for the last thirty-five years and have taken medication twice a day to keep my heart in a regular rhythm all this time. The first medication I was on was changed after twenty years because it was found that patients with my condition that were taking this medication were dropping dead suddenly. OK, I'll make the change. From time to time, when I get a lot of stress or get fatigued, it goes into an irregular rhythm that lasts two or three days. That puts me at risk for a stroke, so I take another medication when that occurs to prevent that. Yesterday, I had to slow down for a day or so to let my heart regain its regular rhythm.

When it was first diagnosed, I was doing large-animal work in northern Vermont. After a long series of days and nights on the road in our busy season, I was resting in front of the TV when I felt my heart start to roll over in my chest and felt like I had a couple of kittens in there rolling around, playing with each other. I got a little light-headed, and I didn't know what was going on, so I checked in to the local emergency at the hospital at 2:00 AM. They admitted me and hooked me up to an IV and an ECG (electrocardiogram). By 6:00 AM I was beginning to worry because I had to be ready to start farm visits by 7:00 AM. The doctors decided to anesthetize me and electroshock my heart with the paddles. I told them I wanted to get up for a minute and walk around. While I was walking, I felt the heart resume its normal rhythm, which I reported to them. They watched my ECG for a few more minutes, then I had them unhook me from the IV and ECG leads. I put on my coveralls and boots and went to work for the day.

After that, whenever I felt the rhythm slip into fibrillation, I would drive up to the emergency room, sometimes at midnight or later, and tell them at the desk why I was there and that I didn't want to be seen or admitted. I just wanted to sit there until my heart converted back to its regular rhythm, but if I lost consciousness, they had my permission to admit me. I would return home in the early morning and prepare to go out on farm calls as my children were getting up for the day, not realizing that I had spent the night at the hospital ER waiting room.

Such was my life in the days of building a practice. We had four children and farm clients depending on me, so I didn't have time to be sick, or rather, I didn't have time to rest and be sick at the same time. Sometimes I would come in late at night from work and look in on the children and wonder if I would live to be old enough for them to remember who I was. I made it! For that I am grateful. Now, when it occurs, I just work through it. The more I work, the less I think and worry about it.

Yesterday I was engrossed in a busy work schedule. My heart had been out of sync for two days. I had a sudden flushed feeling, and I realized that my heart had converted back to its normal rhythm, which always comes as a welcome relief and the same feeling of exhilaration I have when preparing to leave on a weeklong vacation. My father-in-law passed away suddenly from a massive heart attack at the age of forty-nine while I was in veterinary college. I have had four close friends pass away suddenly at early ages between thirty and forty-five. Each of these instances came as a terrible shock. I have been impressed throughout my career with how fragile mortality is, and whenever I begin to take things for granted, an episode of atrial fib reminds me that every day is a blessing.

This morning, I walk into the exam room to the wagging tail of a middle-aged golden retriever. She is a longtime client who loves it when I kneel down to bring my face level with hers. She sniffs me over from head to toe while I wait patiently for her to complete her exam. Then she gives my face a familiar lick or two as though to say, "OK, you are who I remember, go ahead." Then it is my turn to sniff her over head to toe and see if she is healthy. Accompanying her is her owner sitting in a chair with a cane, looking remarkably like my mother, and moving as carefully. Standing across from her is her middle-aged son, who always comes with her now that her husband has passed on a few years ago. He is a nice guy and a good son. His mother greets me with a broad smile as does he, pleasantly surprised to see me walk into the exam room and home from Arizona.

We talk about how their lives are going and how their dog is doing. I recommend to the son that he buy his mother a scooter like the ones I bought for my mother. They changed her life from being housebound to being able to spend several hours at any mall, going from store to store, conversing with salesclerks and seeing all the latest styles and purses. He sounds truly interested, so I google up the scooter store in Florida where I got them and print the pages so he can check it out on his own. His mother is smiling the whole time we are together. My heart is touched as I see my mother in her face. She wants to know how Arizona worked out for us and how Judy is doing with her shoulder and how our diet is going.

When the visit is over, she smiles more broadly and struggles to get up from her chair while her son holds the dog. I grasp her arm to steady her and help her to her feet. She looks me in the eye and says, "I still remember how you came to visit me in the nursing home when I broke my hip." I touch her shoulder and tell her that I remember that day too. It was a special afternoon three years ago that took very little of my time but let her know that I was concerned for her and gave her a pleasant memory that she would carry with her to the next life. For me it was heartwarming to bring such comfort to her at a troubling time in her life with just a small gesture. It bonded us forever. Sometimes I think my veterinary practice is more of a ministry, and that's OK. It's just the way I want it, and I'm glad to be back at it.

Today was, perhaps, one of our busiest days on record. To top it off, we were one doctor short of a full staff, so I left for work early with a comfortable pair of loose-fitting trousers, a short-sleeved loose-fitting shirt, and running shoes. On a busy day, the details count, and the right clothing allows for free and easy movement while kneeling on the floor to be at face level with a patient or to lift one up to the table or to wrestle with one that doesn't want to be there. The day began in the night when an expatriate client who became disgruntled with us two years ago over a clinic policy issue and decided to travel elsewhere for veterinary care showed up at our door unannounced with a small dog that had been severely traumatized and was comatose. My business was about taking care of sick and defenseless animals, not about holding grudges, so I rolled out the red carpet and did everything I could to save this dog. He was a sweet, lovable little guy as it turned out, but lying on our treatment table not able to move or even lift his head, I thought it was his last night on the planet.

Nevertheless, I learned long ago not to write anything off that was still breathing. I quickly hooked up an IV and treated him for shock and hospitalized him for the night. I checked on him two or three times through the night and early morning, and each time I did, he looked a little better. Within a couple of hours, he could hold his head up, and on the second check, he could stand where previously I thought his problem was spinal damage that might be irreversible and cause permanent paralysis. I called the owners before midnight to tell them he was much improved. By midday today he had been out for two walks and had eaten a meal.

At 4:00 AM, a call came in about a seizuring cat, so I had them bring him in. Both animals had improved during the treatment and course of the day today for me to be able to send them home tonight. The afternoon was jam-packed with routine appointments. One hour into the schedule, a family called that had been on the road for nine hours and was traveling through the area. They stopped to let their dog out for a leg stretch. He drank a lot of water very quickly, causing his stomach to bloat and then to twist. When they told me by phone that he was rolling all around and vomiting after gulping down a lot of water, I had my diagnosis without even seeing him. I told them they better got him to the clinic ASAP. When they arrived, James confirmed my "hunchnosis" and took him into surgery for three hours to untwist the stomach and suture it down to the abdominal wall to prevent recurrence.

That left us short of yet another veterinarian for office hours, so we really scrambled for the next three hours. The waiting room was packed with owners and animals. I was grateful for understanding, compassionate, and empathetic owners who kept smiling and patiently waited until we could tend to their beloved pet. It was a stress-filled afternoon but an inspiring one thanks to our clientele. I had my face licked many times, which always had a calming, heartwarming effect on my soul. The owners of the gastric torsion dog came in to visit him after his surgery and were thrilled that he was doing well. It was a two-day delay and detour in their plans and trip, but nonetheless, they were joyous. Thank you, James, for calmly and methodically changing night to day for their best friend. He would be able to finish the journey home with them.

By the close of hours at 5:30 PM, we had completed about 135 appointments. It was an exciting, satisfying, exhilarating day that flew by in the twinkling of an eye and yet, at the same time, seemed to be never ending. This is what I signed up for. So grateful to be Doctor Dan.

A few years ago, when Brent and Danny were playing Little League, we used to go to all their games. We met a man our age who came to the games as well to watch his son. He was a jovial, likable guy, and he taught us the infield fly rule, which we reviewed at each game to make sure I had it right. We became good friends with his family and went out together for dinner a few times. One day he came to visit and took me aside and told me that he was having back pains, so he went to the doctor for X-rays and found he had prostate cancer that had spread into his spine. It was a shocking revelation that he made to me with much emotion. I was at a loss to say anything. He and I both knew that his days would be short on the earth. He asked my advice, and I told him to make the most of every minute he had left. I vowed to myself that I would not desert my friend in his hour of need. We visited him often, and in the last year of his life, we traveled with our children every Wednesday and Sunday some forty-five miles to his house.

At first he could be taken out in a wheelchair, so the boys and I would lift his wheelchair out the door to the street and take him for a walk up the street and back to get him outside and into the fresh air. Later, he became bedridden and could not be moved; the pain was so great. Our young children came each time without complaint and with a compassionate heart. The trips became more and more somber, but they never complained; they always were ready to make the trip and offered no excuses for not going. Toward the end, my friend asked me about how euthanasia worked with animals. He was, in his own way, asking me to finish it for him, and I must admit that the thought of covering his face with a pillow and lying on it crossed my mind. It was a very tough time for me, but my friend carried a far greater burden than I.

I spoke at his funeral and shared the intricacies of the infield fly rule that had brought us together. I wondered what purpose his lingering death had served, and then I thought of the opportunities it gave him and his children to discuss the really serious things of life that they otherwise never would have approached. I thought of my children and Judy who gave so compassionately of their time, friendship, and support to my friend. I was and am so proud of them for their service and for that time that we had together to serve him and console him. It bound us together as servants of our God and fellow man. I saw purpose in his life and in his passing. That was a time of sorrow and sweet service that I will never forget.

I've been watching the weather in Arizona since we left in April. One hundred seventeen degrees is very hot. The hottest I have ever experienced has been standing between two cows at the evening milking after they have come in from being on pasture on a hot summer's day. A cow's normal temperature is 102, but a black-and-white Holstein cow coming in from a day in the hot sun can have a temperature of 106.

In my farm days, I would check over a hundred cows a day by rectal exam to check for pregnancy or palpate the reproductive organs to check for ovarian cysts, uterine infection, and other conditions that might impair breeding, which was critical to the financial health of the farm and, in the long run, to the health of the cow. I could tell instantly if a cow had a normal temperature, since a cow with 106 degree F temperature would cause my arm to feel like it was on fire, compared to the normal 102 F. In the course of checking cows, if I happened onto one that was running a fever, I would ask the farmer if this cow was acting sick. If not, then we would take a few minutes to examine her, and often we would find that she had acute mastitis or mammary infection that had just occurred since the last milking. Mastitis cases treated early would respond much better to treatment and had a better chance of returning to full production than ones found later in the day or week.

One evening, I was checking a cow that came in off pasture and was acting very sick. When I took her temperature, it read over 110 F degrees. This cow had been running a fever of 105 F to 106 F over the last ten days, and nothing we gave her seemed to make a difference. I couldn't believe she was still alive, much less still standing. I thought of how I could rapidly decrease her temperature before the proteins in her body started to congeal like scrambled eggs. I had the farmer get some towels, soaked them in cold water, and draped them over the cow. Then I started an IV with cold Lactated Ringer's flowing as fast as I could get it to go into the jugular vein.

After ten minutes, her temperature had only dropped a degree. I racked my brain for another way to get her temperature down. I watched the hired man hand-stripping the udder of a cow with mastitis into a three-gallon stainless steel milking pail, but my mind was elsewhere, racing to find a way to save this cow. Then, inspiration!

I grabbed the pail from the hired man, dumped out the mastitis milk, washed the pail out, and filled it with cold water. I got my stomach tube from the truck. A stomach tube for a cow is about the same circumference as a garden hose, only it's stiffer and rounded off at the end so it can be safely passed down the esophagus (of the cow) without causing any damage to the mucous membranes but stiff enough to be able to push it along to the stomach. If I siphoned the cold water into the rumen (stomach), it would be lost in the huge amount of hay and ingesta and do little to drop the cow's temperature. So I chose the other end. I put on a shoulder-length glove/sleeve and filled the stomach tube with water after suspending the pail full of water from baler string tied over the barn support beam that ran the length of the barn over the tails of the cows in their stanchions. The other end of the stomach tube was being held in the pail of water by the farmer while I took my end in rectally as far as my arm would reach, up to about her kidneys. Then I took my finger off the end of the stomach tube, and the three gallons of cold water siphoned quickly into this feverish intestine, cooling the abdomen.

Every morning as I prepare to leave home for work, I offer a silent prayer, asking my Father in heaven to help me in my work. In this case, I said an extra prayer that this would work. Within a half hour, her temperature was normal and never went up again. Cows never say thank-you and are usually frightened and alarmed by the procedures we use to treat them. Nevertheless, I take great satisfaction in seeing a contented cow standing in her stall, eating her grain eagerly, with an udder full of milk, where previously she stood staring ahead with her grain lying in a pile in front of her, untouched. Cows and me, we be buds. That's not a sentiment I ever remotely thought I would have growing up a city boy. The course of my life, as I review it, is a miracle to me. That I would have the privilege of working among my four-legged friends as my life's work is more than I ever hoped for or even dreamed of and, in my humble opinion and testimony, not a chance happening.

Last Night in Arizona for a Few Months

Softly falls the light of day as our campfire fades away. Silently, each one should ask, Have I done my daily task? Have I done and have I dared everything to be prepared? Have I kept my honor bright? Can I guiltlessly sleep tonight? *Boy Scout Vesper*

It has been a wonderful few months here in Arizona with time to look back, to enjoy the present as never before, and to look to the future. I have had time to reflect, time to encourage, time to lend a helping hand, time to listen, and time to console. The human spirit can be so inspiring, and it can be so evil. The choice is ours to make.

Each of us has made poor choices from time to time, but each new day is the start of the rest of our lives, and looking to the future, we move ahead with hope for a better day. Some lessons we learn come the hard way. When I first began practicing large-animal medicine, I was so enthralled by the work I was doing that I paid no attention to what effect I was having on those around me. I stood in line at the post office one afternoon after a strenuous day of wrestling cows and heifers in close quarters. The man ahead of me approached the counter and asked in a loud voice, "Are you guys mailing calves now? It smells like a barn in here." The postmaster replied, "No, sir, but there's a veterinarian standing right behind you." He turned and stared at me and turned three shades of red while I turned a shade of red of my own. "I didn't mean anything by it, Doc. I love the smell of a barn."

In those days, I wore white coveralls to work. They called me Mr. Clean. I kept about three pairs with me and changed often. The day before, I dehorned calves all morning. I had some blood on my coveralls after my efforts, which took on a conspicuous look against the background of my white coveralls. I also carried the scent of "eau de corral" with me. I stopped at a small café for lunch. As I began to eat my dinner, a man and his wife got up from their table and brushed by, glaring at me, and went to the check out. In a loud voice for all the patrons to hear he explained to the cashier that he was leaving his dinner half-eaten because this so-called educated man (me) came in covered in blood and stinking the place up and caused him to lose his appetite. I just kept on chewing my cud at my table, ignoring his outburst, but I was pretty embarrassed and felt bad that I had been oblivious to my appearance and smell and their effects on the patrons of the restaurant. The whole room became suddenly silent as the spotlight shone on me. The silence was broken by a jovial, kindhearted man who said, laughing, "That guy is just showing his ignorance—calling a man from Cornell educated." I decided that now was not the time to stand up for my alma mater, the Ontario Veterinary College. The lesson of the day did not go unnoticed though. I always washed up and changed coveralls before going in to lunch from that day on.

When I was practicing large-animal medicine, we didn't have GPS or cell phones.

We had road maps and a two-way radio, with a thirty-foot radio tower at the house where the base station was. I was known as Mobile One. After each farm visit was done, I would drive my truck to the highest point around and call in with "Mobile one to base" to get the new calls that had come in. I was in Morris one afternoon driving away from my latest farm call when I heard the radio crackle, "Base to mobile two, Morris-Mini farm just called. They have a miniature horse trying to deliver her foal but not getting anywhere. They need assistance right away, but they said don't send Gilchrist, his arm is too big." I answered back, "I got your message, but I'm right next to their farm, so I'll stop in to see what I can do." I pulled up to their barn, got out of the truck, and watched their faces fall when they saw it was me. *Too bad, folks, I'm all you've got today, but get out of my way, keep your eyes open and your mouths shut,* I thought, but what I said was, "I know you think my arm is too big, but my partner is an hour away, and I'm right here. If you wait for him, the foal and maybe the mare will be dead by the time he gets here, so let's see what we can do." If I could get my oversized forearm into a small ewe and manipulate a tiny lamb and get it out, I believed I could do this.

I had them get lots of hot water. I prepared my arm with lots of lubricant as I washed up the mare. She was lying on her side, straining like a son of a gun, but that was par for the course. I slowly put my hand inside, stretching the tissue as I went. I found a tiny nose at my fingertips about ten inches inside. I followed along under her chin up to her neck. By now I was in up to the middle of my forearm, and darn it, they were right—my arm was big. But at the foal's neck, I felt the hooves just at the tips of my fingers, and that was about as far as I could go. I pushed my arm as hard as I could to get in enough to grasp one tiny hoof with my fingertips. I pinched it as hard as I could and pulled it up under the foal's chin until I could move my fingers above the hoof and get a good grip on the leg then pull it under the chin extended to its full length and protruding outside through the vulva. Then I repeated the procedure with the other hoof and leg. They were about the size of large celery sticks. Once both hooves were outside, I put my fingers in the foal's nostrils, pulling the head simultaneously with the feet, and presto, within ten minutes of arriving, we had a live, flopping, glorious tiny foal on the straw behind the mare, who was getting her feet under her and preparing to rise up and take over reviving her foal. Ha, I did it! The owners were amazed and deliriously happy.

In this business, success says it all, so nothing else needed to be said. From that day on, they never asked for me not to be sent again. And every time I went back there for the next three years, I always asked how that mare and foal were doing, reminding them in my own subtle way of their request that day, not to have me come. I have learned over the years to focus on the things I can do and not to even think of the things I can't do. And the main thing I can do, the strength I have that has built my practice, is to try. Never give up; there is always a way. But the real cornerstone of my practice upon which I have fully relied and depended over the years is my faith in my Father in heaven. Each morning as I headed out on the roads on my way to my first call of the day and even now on my way to the clinic, I said and say a prayer asking for inspiration and guidance to do the best I can do. In my darkest hour and in the jubilation of success, I have never forgotten nor lost my faith. I love Job's response to his wife when all appeared lost and he was at his lowest low, covered from head to foot with boils, when she said, "Dost thou still retain thine integrity? Curse God, and die." He replied, "What kind of a servant would I be if I only praised God when times were good?" Veterinary medicine has truly blessed my life as it has drawn me closer to my

Maker. Thank you, Lord, for everything I have experienced in life, both good and bad. Thank you for caring enough to let me find my way.

Motherhood is an inspiring calling, no matter what the species. Two mothers in my own life, my own and my wife, have taken me down paths that I would never otherwise have ventured and have helped me find my way. Their experiences and how they have responded to them and carried on through difficult times have strengthened my resolve to move ahead, unwavering from the path they walk, and to lend my support to them wherever I can. My mother writes this:

> In 1953, we had a beautiful baby boy born to us. I couldn't believe how perfect he was and he touched everyone's heart. People would say about him, there is something special about that child. And I would hold him and look at him and my eyes were often wet with tears and I would say to him 'Oh please don't die and leave me, I can't bare it if you die.' When he was three months old, he died of meningitis. I couldn't understand it. We had done everything expected of us and the Lord had let me down. We put our arms around each other and shared out grief. Sharing in a marriage is important in good times and bad. But then I thought of my experience when I was converted to the gospel, and I knew by all the things people had experienced on seeing the boy and my own feelings that he would die that our Heavenly Father's plan had been in place and accepted His hand in my life.

I was only three when this happened, but I remember a little of it. I know that my mother never wavered in her faith in the ensuing years and that her love for me was a constant in my life, never influenced by the grief she experienced. I really never realized how much she was affected by the loss of her child until thirteen years later when we traveled west on vacation and one day visited the grave of my little brother. She broke down in tears on seeing his name on the gravestone, and it was only then that I witnessed her grief. Her love for each of us was and always will be a major driving force and influence in our lives.

These past years, I watched Judy suffer unrelenting deep bone pain in her shoulder that allowed her sleep for only one or two hours at a time and often went over twenty-four hours before sleep overrode pain and she drifted into unconsciousness. We had tried everything we could think of to offer relief but to no avail. Then two years ago, we discovered Arizona on a visit to my brother Mike. In the course of that visit, we suddenly realized that one pain-free day led to another. This past winter in Arizona, I watched Judy sleep through the night, awaken refreshed and ready to enjoy life, and enthusiastically face each day as an adventure of discovery.

In April, she boarded the plane that took her back to unrelenting pain, but she didn't hesitate to do it. She had children and grandchildren and one on the way to come back to. She had sewing for them that awaited her arrival. She had grown daughters who needed to sit on her lap and feel their mother's love and grandchildren who yearned for her touch. Their draw overrode the knowledge that pain and suffering awaited her return. Like an old enemy, the pain gripped her as we headed east, not even waiting until the plane landed to set in. The first week was terrible until her body once again became accustomed to the constant pain that a plate and screws in her shoulder emanated. Nevertheless, her heart dictated her actions, not her body. For this alone she holds my undying admiration and devotion. Whither thou goest I will go.

I call my mother daily and visit her as often as I can, and I try to do as much as I can to offer support and care and sympathy for Judy. I hope that they regard each day of their life as Mother's Day. It is for me.

The terrible floods this summer in Oncida were the worst I have experienced, so when the call went out for help in cleanup, I decided to devote a week to doing what I could to assist in cleanup.

Today I worked in damp, humid cellars that reeked of sewer gas. I did OK with it, having a strong stomach from seeing and working on some pretty putrid things in the veterinary field (gangrene, festering tumors, maggot infestations, to name a few), none of which caused any kind of nausea in me. At about 1:00 PM, some kind people came around the neighborhood delivering hamburgers, pizza, and fluids for the workers. I was invited to partake, but I learned a long time ago that stench and dinner didn't mix. At least not in my case. Quite a few years ago, I was called out to deliver a calf. When I arrived, I discovered that the farmer had been watching this cow for a few days, and since she wasn't making any headway delivering her calf after four days of being in labor, he thought he'd better call. He thought right, albeit seventy-two hours later than he should have had this epiphany. I listened to his story after arriving and had a few choice words for him in my mind, but my mouth said, "OK, well, let's wash her up and check to see what's going on."

What was going on was that she had a calf inside that had been dead for three days, and it had begun to swell up with gas. The calf's head and limbs were swelled up twice their normal size, and the wonderful lubricating amniotic fluid that allowed for a slick and relatively easy delivery was long gone. The calf was dry and swollen, and it was my job to get it out of there or the mother was a dead cow. A caesarean section was out of the question since the inside of her uterus was full of rotten, putrid, infected material that would leak into her abdomen if I opened the uterus and took the calf surgically. It would be the cow's death warrant. A natural delivery with the calf coming out intact would never work now. Three days ago, yes, but now, no. The calf was way too swollen to ever pass through the birth canal. That left but one choice—getting the calf out in pieces. It had been dead for three days, so this procedure was the only way. I won't go into the gory details, but as I worked for the next three hours to effect the delivery, my arm was in up to my shoulder, and the cow was straining every thirty seconds or so. Whenever she strained, the gas that was accumulating in her uterus would expel in a warm breeze over my face. It was the putrid smell of decaying tissues, like the smell of rotten eggs. None of this caused me any upset as I worked steadily and methodically toward completing the task at hand.

I arrived midmorning and completed my task by 1:00 or 1:30 PM. I washed up my arms and equipment and changed my coveralls and headed down the road to my next call. I carried the stench of the morning in my nostrils and deeply embedded into the first few layers of skin on my arms. I was getting a little hungry, but I was in a hurry to get onto the next farm, being a little behind from the prolonged calving. I stopped at a general store and bought a drink, a packet of sliced Swiss cheese, and a package of sliced salami. I opened that salami and put a slice into my mouth. It was heavily spiced, and it tasted too similar to the stench I had just left. I almost lost it then as I pulled over to the side of the road and spat out what was in my mouth and pitched the remainder of the salami as far as I could into the pasture next to me. I fasted for the rest of the day and then ate something very bland for supper: white toast and jam with no butter.

Those were days and lessons I shall never forget, and from time to time, I get a flashback as I did today coming out of the cellar to the offer of lunch. I was grateful today and yesterday that Judy accompanied me and busied herself working with the members of the Salvation Army, helping the lost souls of the flood. She comforted the weary and gave hope to the hopeless. She offered a listening, sympathetic ear and shed more than a tear or two at their stories. She helped one family find accommodations starting tomorrow when they lose their berths at the YMCA, and she helped a discouraged, distraught gentleman to his home, carrying a gallon of bleach for him. She was a true angel of mercy, and she had a compassionate smile for us when we returned to base filthy, smelly, tired, and inspired. She was a welcome sight at the end of the day.

Rain, rain, rain, and more rain. The fields are lush and green and wet. It's plenty warm here, but it's a wet heat. Judy's shoulder is on fire 24-7. If I only could, I would give her one of my shoulders and take on her pain. As it is, I can only sympathize and try to cheer her up. This rain forest brings to mind a call I had in 1978 for a down cow trying to have her calf in the middle of a river. When I arrived, we drove my truck down to the water's edge. Sure enough, there was a cow in the river unable to get up and almost knee-deep in water. I washed her up and examined her to see how the calf was doing. She was empty. No calf, just a postcalving uterus. The farmer and I looked up and down the shore but no calf.

I surmised she must have delivered her calf in the water, and the river current took it away. She was heavy enough and unable to get up, so she sat there on the river's edge like an anchor. I tied up her head and gave her a 500 cc bottle of calcium IV to restore the calcium levels that had dropped postcalving, causing her paralysis. As I was finishing up the IV, I heard the faint blat of a newborn calf. I looked all around to no avail. Then I looked across the river to the distant bank on the other side, and there lying in the meadow bordering the stream was her calf calling for her mother and her first meal. I couldn't believe it. Somehow that calf had managed to swim across the current to the other side and pulled itself up the bank to firm ground and safety. At least for the moment.

The farmer had to get a boat to go fetch her while I coaxed the cow to try to arise. One more bleat from her calf after the jolt of a bottle of calcium IV was all the stimulus she needed to arise and walk. We both were soaked, but it was a glorious moment. I packed my things, changed into some dry coveralls, put on my saturated boots, and headed down the highway to my next call. Those days were full, varied, intriguing, and inspiring.

On one occasion, after just such a day, I returned home late into the night. I ate a cold dinner left on the counter by my wife with instructions to nuke it (microwave) to warm it up, but I was too tired and hungry to bother, so I ate it cold, and I ate it ravenously. As I ate, I went through the mail of the day. One letter caught my eye and filled me with apprehension. It was an official envelope from the USDA (United States Department of Agriculture). As I opened it, I recognized a health chart I had filled out a few days earlier for a group of cattle going to Canada. It needed the endorsement of the federal veterinarian before they could leave. It was endorsed, which was a relief to me, because those certificates need to have every *i* dotted and every *t* crossed to earn the sacred signature of the federal veterinarian. A sticky note was attached to the document with a critique telling me that my health certificate carrying three lengthy required statements regarding the health status of the animals in question was hand printed and contained a couple of spelling errors. These certificates, it said, appear more professional if they are typed and carefully proofread. Although the veterinarian signed it, they informed me that this certificate was the most unprofessional document they had ever endorsed.

I read the note as I swallowed my last forkful of dinner. I took a large gulp of milk to wash it down. Then I dropped the letter on the floor and did a rain dance on it. Unprofessional? Perhaps. But I'll tell you something, my friend. When my phone rings on any day of the year at anytime of the day or night, as the song says, "I'll be there." If you own an animal in my practice, you are never alone. In my world, there is nothing more professional than a person who cheerfully rolls up their sleeves and gets to work when called upon *no matter what time or day it is.* I have been waiting twenty-five years to get this off my chest. Thank you for your attention.

Today started out very stressfully. We had over 160 appointments scheduled at the clinic. There were five veterinarians working all morning, including myself. At noon, Mallory, granddaughter Cady, and I traveled to Oneida to join Judy, who went earlier, working again in providing relief to the flood victims there. I was given the assignment of knocking on doors of a few houses to see what their needs were. As I passed one house, I watched a group of Mennonites working to strip floors and tear out Sheetrock so things could dry out before rebuilding. The young men looked at me with broad grins and asked if I remembered them. I asked if they were related to one of my Mennonite farmers I used to go to. "He's our father" came the reply. "Then I remember you" was my response. "You were three feet tall back then, and now you are all grown-up!" When I finished house to house, I returned to where they were working and shoveled Sheetrock and lathing alongside them all afternoon. It was wonderful to be working with them again after all these years. I told the homeowner who was working with us that I used to be their farm vet and that they were my best farmers. Then the father exclaimed, "He is the best veterinarian ever," which touched me since I hadn't spoken to him in over ten years. For friends at first are friends again at last.

Earlier in the afternoon, I stopped at one house to ask their needs. A young man in his twenties said they were all set; they just needed an electrician to get their power going. He was a renter, but he said someone stole a new washer and dryer his father had purchased for him six days before the flood and which he put in the front yard to dry out. Looters also stole his and his wife's new bikes and bicycle trailer to house their four-month-old newborn. I expressed outrage that someone would do that when they had already suffered so much loss, then he left to go to his family, and I went to work with the Mennonites. I thought all afternoon about that young man and his bride. It is an early age to be so disappointed by our fellow man. He impressed me with his positive attitude and his work ethic as evidenced by the postflood cleanup at his place. I had his phone number in my pocket, so I called him and asked more about the items he lost. Then I told him I would like to replace the washer and dryer and bikes. He couldn't speak—he was so emotional—and neither could I, so there was a long period of silence. Then I was able to ask where he bought the items. I went to his appliance store and purchased the washer and dryer, and they promised to keep it until he was ready and then deliver it and hook it up. Then I met him and his wife and baby at Walmart to purchase the bikes and trailer. It was an emotional meeting, and both he and his wife had trouble speaking as we picked out their bikes. Then we loaded them in my truck and took them over to his father's, where they were staying. I visited with his father a few minutes, and then we hugged as I left. As I was pulling out, the young couple was standing in the driveway hugging and crying. It was moving to me that I found them today and, perhaps, restored their faith in mankind. Thank you, Lord, for leading me to them and for opening my eyes to see, my ears to listen, and my heart to act.

I just returned from the clinic. Our night watchman is on duty. I can sleep in peace.

I stopped for a softdrink at the quick stop. The last time I pulled in there, a man about my age approached me and began talking to me. He knew I was a veterinarian, and he had plenty of stories about wild animals he had encountered in his travels around the countryside. It looked like he spent a lot of time in his old truck. I was dog tired and had a hard time keeping my eyes open while he described in great detail his last week living on the road. I tried to think of a way I could politely excuse myself and go home to bed. Then I realized by the length and breadth of his stories that I was probably the only human being he had talked to today and, perhaps, in many days or at least the only one who listened. It's a sad world sometimes—all of us in a hurry to go somewhere or get home to our families and no time for fellowship with a lonely stranger. I thought as he talked that my obligation tonight was to listen to him and to take mental notes of what he was saying and to ask pertinent questions that would show him I was listening and I was interested. And I was, on both counts. I think a lot of the violence that goes on around us and even up to our very doorsteps is in part because no one listens to the next man anymore. I went to bed a little later than planned and got a little less sleep, but I was happy that I heard and followed a prompting to be a friend to a lonely soul. That might be me someday, and on some occasions, it is.

Sometimes in life, it's worth whatever you have to do to arrange things. Today I took my father to meet my friend Jack. Jack drove a tank in World War II and always asked about my father (a World War II bomber pilot) when I went to visit him. He remembered the role the bombers played in pounding the German tanks and infantry before he had to move ahead into enemy territory. Today, some sixty-eight years later, my dad and he shook hands and visited. Jack played his harmonica for Dad as we sat in his humble living room / bedroom, then Dad took one of his harmonicas and played "God Save the Queen." Both men were deaf and could hardly walk. I had to yell in their ears to tell the other what was said. Jack related that when the bombers (such as the one my father piloted) flew over after bombing the Germans, they would tip their wings back and forth to say good-bye and the coast was clear. As we shuffled down the stairs to leave, Jack called to my dad. As Dad turned to look, Jack tipped his arms back and forth in similitude of the pilots' signal so many years ago that all was well. It was a touching moment to see these old warriors meet after so many years. Jack said forlornly to Dad that all his old buddies were gone now, to which Dad nodded in agreement and said, "So are mine. But," he said, "they still can't get rid of us." Nobility at its finest. True gentlemen that are my privilege to know.

It's a beautiful day in central New York or, as we say in the queen's English, "Beauty eh." Today a man came in to return some medications. His canine friend had cancer, and he just found out that his wife did as well. He was on the verge of tears as he told his story. His dog and his wife both had cancer. He said this couldn't have come at a worse time in his life. I was at a loss as to what I could say that might offer him some comfort other than

"Sometimes life just sneaks up behind us and bites us on the rear end." Then I felt moved to put my hand on his shoulder and tell him this was his chance to shine. It was his opportunity to be a knight in shining armor for his wife. I closed our appointment with an emotional expression of sorrow to him for his troubles. I hope he sees his opportunity for service to his wife. It could really be their sweetest time together.

Spring in Waterville, New York. It is the one time of year I miss being on the road traveling from farm to farm. The earth is waking from her Sabbath-day rest, and old friends are rising from their beds to blossom. I feel excitement in the air as I cross a babbling brook while driving down an isolated country road. Adventure beckons me from years past, inviting me to pack my duffel bag and hit the open road in search of what comes next. But duty says there are things to do here and loved ones to care of and obligations to fulfill. And I'm OK with that. I have no regrets, just a spirit that dreams of days gone by. I am happy in my work. O Danny boy, the pipes, the pipes are calling, from glen to glen and down the mountainside. I hear.

Yesterday we helped son-in-law Garrett, who graduated from Southern Virginia University and had been accepted at veterinary college in Grenada, and daughter Mallory, who also graduated two years ago from SVU, pack everything they owned into a 6 × 12 U-haul, our pickup, and the trunk of their car, preparing for a great adventure ahead, leaving behind cherished friends, a cozy home in a quiet, safe, beautiful village in the picturesque hills of Virginia, and a university that had cared and nurtured, educated, and employed them for the last six years. I felt their apprehension. It is a journey of faith and courage that lay ahead. As we were finishing, their landlord and his friend stopped in to say good-bye. He was a kindly gentleman in his eighties, who lost the love of his life when she passed a few short years ago. He was not a member of our church, but as he prepared to leave, he asked if we could all form a circle and have a word of prayer, which he offered. In that prayer, he gave thanks to the Lord for knowing Garrett and Mallory and said that they were the finest people he had met. He expressed in his prayer hope that they would call him from time to time and blessed them on their journey. He brought tears to all who stood there with him. It was a humble, touching prayer of the heart from a weathered, elderly man whose life had been touched often with sadness but whose spirit had been lifted and strengthened by his association with this young couple.

Humanity at its finest and true nobility in that humble cottage in an obscure village in the beautiful Virginia mountains. It was well worth the drive here and back just to be a part of that circle. Thank you, Mallory and Garrett, for being such good tenants and caring friends to an elderly saint that he would offer such a prayer. Thank you, Lord, for bringing me here to this fine place to witness this scene. It was touching and inspiring. Congratulations, Garrett, on graduating from SVU and being accepted at St. George University College of Veterinary Medicine, but far more importantly, congratulations to this young couple for distinguishing yourselves in the school of life. I have learned today from both of you.

I just learned this evening that one of my old farm clients passed away. He was a rough, tough guy, always looking for a fight. If he was angry with me (say, if I got to his farm to take care of his cows too close to milking time), he would stand up close to me with his belly touching mine and his face two inches from my nose and speak in a loud, garlic-laden voice, telling me off. I gave it right back to him, never backing down, always ready for a knuckle sandwich, which he was known around town to readily dish out. One morning, I came to his barn, and he met me just outside his milk house. He grabbed my hand to shake it, so I shook back. But he wouldn't let go, and he started to squeeze it, and when I looked him in the eye, he gave me a satanic grin. I smiled back and squeezed back. Neither of us said a word for two minutes, but he started to sweat, and his grin disappeared as he dropped to his knees and finally let go. I've wrestled bigger, tougher bulls than this and never left the job undone. After that, he never got in my face again. I later learned that when he was a teenager, his father suffered a tragic death. In spite of his meanness, I always had a soft spot in my heart for this man, knowing all that he had been through. There are many sad stories out there that go untold. I have a few myself. Judge not that ye be not judged, for by what judgment ye judge, ye shall be judged. Matthew 7:1-2. Rest in peace, my friend.

My friend Jack lost his dog four weeks ago. She died at home. I gave her to him when she was eight weeks old and took care of her medical needs for the last thirteen years. I call him once every two or three weeks to visit with him, and lately, since his dog died, I have been visiting him at his home. Jack is eighty-seven and a veteran of World War II. He had lost many friends and pets over the years, but this one was especially hard for a man who felt all alone in the world. Two nights ago, some brothers from church and my grandson and I went to his home to sing for him. There were eleven or twelve of us. We brought a dinner that my wife, Judy, prepared for him. We sang two songs he had never heard before from our church hymnbook. His face was illuminated by our songs. Not by the words or by the tunes, but by the brotherhood, sympathy, and spirit of fellowship that we all felt as we crowded into his tiny living room to bring some cheer to my lonely friend. Most of the men had never met him but came with me at my request to fulfill this mission. I thanked them for giving of their time to sing for someone they knew not. It was an indication of their spirits that they came willingly and cheerfully. We sang to let Jack know that he was not alone. We sang to drive out his loneliness. We sang because we are brothers.

Last Christmas, we resurrected the band we began when our children were young and all playing instruments in school. At that time, we were concerned that our children regarded Christmas and life in general as a time to receive. They had long lists of things that they saw on advertisements on television and decided they needed. Judy and I tried to find a way to help them see the joy of giving—not just material goods but, more importantly, of one's time and the good that came of sharing. We came up with the idea of forming a band of brass instruments and playing Christmas carols to some isolated farm clients and church members that we knew. I ordered the sheet music and began practicing with them. I played flügelhorn, James on the trombone, Erin on trumpet, Danny on percussion, and Brent on trombone. Mallory was as yet unborn. Judy made us Christmas sweatshirts and hats, and we picked six or so families to visit.

The day before going, we made cookies and packed them up as Christmas plates. We called ourselves the Canadian Brats. I bet they never had a farm visit like that before from their veterinarian. It was a huge success and became a family tradition until the children began leaving home and our band disbanded. Last year, we began again—this time with our grandchildren, who were now playing instruments. Erin rejoined us with her trumpet, and Mallory came with us with her beautiful voice. We traveled to one of our people who lived in a nursing home. It was just after dinner, and we found him in the dining room with some of the other residents. We played two carols with our instruments, then Mallory sang "Silent Night" a cappella. She sang with the voice of an angel. One elderly gentleman in a wheelchair became annoyed and yelled out, "Shut up. You have a terrible voice. Your voice is killing my ears." She sang on unwavering with a smile on her face. I clenched my teeth in anger and frustration and looked away, trying to concentrate on Mallory's song. Soon I noticed that he wasn't making any more disturbance.

During the last verse of "Silent Night," I looked over toward him and saw our oldest daughter, Erin, kneeling by his wheelchair, holding his hand, and listening to the misfortunes in his life that brought him here. In the background, I heard Mallory singing, "Radiant beams from thy holy face, With the dawn of redeeming grace, Jesus, Lord at thy birth, Jesus Lord at thy birth." Thank you, my daughters, for your bravery, generosity, and compassion. Quiet heroes of mine.

Today we were chastised by a client who had to wait for his visit last time, so he left in anger. It was a day of many emergencies that needed immediate attention. He rescheduled his visit to this afternoon, when he was our first appointment. He is considering going to another clinic because we are getting too busy. We have been his veterinarians for several years now, so it dismayed me that he would take such a hard line approach. In other years, we adjusted our schedule to take care of his animals' needs when they required immediate attention. Fortunately our other clientele that day were very compassionate, understanding and happy that we handled things the way we did. Living beings are fragile and unpredictable in some cases, so although we are much less stressed by following a fixed schedule, many are alive today because we are willing to scrap the schedule at a moment's notice to take care of an emergency. I was thinking tonight of my days on the road doing farm visits when I was practicing alone. I arrived one morning at a farm near Cooperstown at 11 AM after telling the farmer I would be there around 9. He was pretty irate. He called to have me check some cows for pregnancy, so I figured I would be there for 45 minutes to an hour. I apologized for being late, but explained I was held up by a difficult calving at the previous farm. The whole time I was checking cows, he was complaining about being behind in his schedule because of my late arrival. As we moved along, he would say ok, I also want you to check this cow's foot. She has been limping on it for the last few days. Then he would find another cow with a foot problem on down the line, he asked me to look at. Finally, as I saw my planned schedule for the day going down the drain by these added tasks, I stopped and said" You know, you were angry because I was late this morning, and I'm happy to check these other cows, but you didn't mention them when you called to have me come this morning, so this is why I was late coming here today and why I'll be late arriving at the next farm, because the last farm also added in some jobs that threw my schedule off." He wasn't too happy with me and grumbled that I must have it pretty good to be complaining about work. I quickly saw that I was on a treadmill getting nowhere if I continued this conversation, so I just bit my tongue and completed the tasks at hand and went on my way. I was young then, with a young family and a huge debt load, so I bit my tongue a lot, and then when I got back into my truck and headed down the highway, I blew my stack and said all the things I wanted to say at the time but held back. By the time I got to the next farm, I had cooled down and was back to my cheerful self. Most of my farm clients were kind, considerate, sympathetic men and women who I regarded as brothers and sisters, so that saw me through the difficult times. Now, older and wiser and free of debt, I still bite my tongue when confrontation rears its ugly head. I have learned to wait and hold my tongue and contemplate a little and cool down. A kind word will make more friends than any other approach. It's funny how life goes. The things you buck at and resist, but do because circumstances demand that you do when you are young and broke, prove to be the best approach when you arrive at a point in life when more dire options are open to you.

Today (Saturday) was a work day. I'm on call until Monday. We had office hours from 8 AM until 1:30, then it's all mine until Monday morning. At 6 PM, I joined my brothers from church in Utica for a spaghetti supper preceeding the general broadcast of Church conference from Salt Lake City. It was good to sit with my brethren and visit and share stories and fellowship as brothers on the path of life. 15 minutes in to the conference and I was on my way back to Waterville for an old dog that was having trouble breathing. I regret none of today. It was an inspiring day and evening. Last week, a young man brought his german shepherd in after he had been hit by a car. He was in tough shape and had a dislocated hip. We took him right in and started an iv, did blood work, treated him for shock and made a place for him to be comfortable and recover. Two days later he was doing fine so we called the young man who owned him and told him he could go home. When he arrived, he had no method of payment, no checking account and no credit. He became irate when we told him we couldn't release the dog without payment. He exclaimed in a loud voice for all to hear what a rip off it was and he guessed we could just keep the dog. He was true to his word, and a week later, we still had the dog. By now, he was beloved of our whole staff. He was starting to use his bad leg, which continued to pop in and out of joint and probably will require surgery. At night, the watchmen let him out to roam around the clinic all night, but he quickly settles down to lie at their feet in the reception room. When I come in to check on things he runs over to me and sniffs me over head to toe and gives me a face lick. Last night we went into the kennel room to check on some patients. Linco told the dog to sit and stay in the reception area. As we were doing our work in the kennel room we looked over to the hallway from the reception and our dog was peeping around the corner to watch us, from a distance. It touched my heart to see his obedience and yet how torn he was between that and wanting to be with us. He is a loveable, quiet, tough, unpretentious canine and we love him. We called the owner Monday and told him that he could come and get him, realizing that payment was probably never going to happen. By Saturday he still hadn't come for him, so after hours today I went to his house to talk turkey. I was angry that after all we had done, he was giving us the run around and even speaking harshly with us for expecting to be paid. I knocked at his door. I heard a dog bark from inside, and then the curtain over the door was pulled aside and the young man looked to see who was there, closed the curtain and a few seconds later emerged from the rear of the house. I told him who I was (not having met him when his dog was admitted) and asked him if he wanted to relinquish his rights to his dog to one of our staff who has become very attached to him. His attitude was completely different than the first time he came in. He apologized for not coming for him and not being able to pay. He said he wanted to call us, but his phone had been cut off, and he has fallen on hard times. My indignant attitude softened as I listened to this young man speak humbly and apologetically of his circumstances. I felt remorse for my feelings toward him and my heart was touched with compassion for him. I've been around the block a time or two and been stiffed by experts for tens of thousands of dollars over the years, and yet something about him told me to go softly. He explained that he just didn't have the money to take care of getting his leg fixed. I told him I was sorry for his troubles but that I could take this problem from him and relieve him at least of that responsibility, to which he readily agreed. So our clinic dog has a new home and a new future and his former owner's burden has been lightened a little. But somehow as I've thought about that young man all day, and the look in his eyes this morning it just doesn't seem enough. He spoke matter-of-factly of his status, not offering excuse or detail other than his phone being cut off, and seemed resigned to his fate. I began to admire his courage. I've been there before, when everything seems to go wrong and there are kids to feed and clothe and shelter to pay for and a job that just provides so much. Tomorrow, on the Sabbath, I will knock on his door once more, and ask him what his troubles are, and see if there is some way I can help. I don't know how bad off he is; the least I can do is offer a listening ear and advice, but perhaps I can do more.

I never get sick. I have worked years in pneumonia traps, been cut with filthy hoof knives and had my partner suture me, been kicked, bitten and stapled myself up, fallen on, stepped on and squished by 1500 pound animals. The last two days my head is so full, water is coming out of my eyes and someone left the tap on in my nose. I've been sneezing and coughing like old faithful, every 5 minutes. I have the cold that has been going around our clinic. Two of our veterinarians are gone for the next 5 days, so not going in to work is not an option. I woke up at 3:30 this morning with a throbbing headache so I got dressed and went in to the clinic to check on the animals, visit with our night watchman and do some paper work. I thought today, I would just be lucky to survive it. But once in the doors, there was no time to feel sorry for myself or lick my wounds. Work jumped at me and there was nowhere to go. At the conclusion of the morning, a couple my age came in with their dog. After treating their buddy, I learned that the wife had just retired from teaching. She taught religious studies in elementary school. I explained that all of our children attended a scripture study class every morning for an hour from 6-7 AM at our church before going to school, all four years that they attended high school. I thought that it was the most important hour of each of their days. The world taught them its ways all day long, and we only had that one hour to show them another side of things, with unconditional love. It brought to mind years of memories of waking them at 5 AM and getting them ready, and driving them in, then waiting for them in the parking lot, and then taking them back. Judy was often their driver, so I could get in to work. As this couple prepared to leave, I took them in to our preparation room at the clinic and showed them two of my favorite pictures. One was a drawing given to me by a friend, of Jesus, laughing. The other was a print of a painting of a lamb and a lion together. She understood the significance of both of them. I thanked her for her career and expressed my admiration for her work with our youth. What a fulfilling career she must have had and a feeling of satisfaction as she now moves forward. The last call of the day at 7 PM was from a man and his son who found an old Labrador up to his chest in mud somewhere in the surrounding hills. He called to see what he should do. I told him to bring him in and then call the police to tell them of his find and where the dog was in case someone called looking for him. The old dog came in weak, cold, shaking and with 2 inches of heavy mud from head to toe. Our staff took charge, and went to work giving him a warm bath and cleaning him up. I started him on antibiotics, and they put him on a pile of warm towels in a cage, with some canned food and water.

He was the dog who came in from the cold. It's midnight and I'm going up to check on him. My cold is still here, but miraculously, I feel good. It was a great day.

I was born and raised to adult hood in Canada. My roots are in the west, but my home is in the East where most of my childhood memories are. For the last 36 years, my professional life as a veterinarian has been within the boundaries of the eastern United States, mostly central New York. As new veterinarians have joined the practice and management has been turned over to other hands, I have had the time to reflect on these many years that have gone by in the twinkling of an eye, but in the day to day business of living, seemed endless. As pain has relentlessly gripped Judy over the last 15 years with unforgiving steadfastness, the discovery of a 75 mile radius pain free zone around Mesa Arizona for Judy came as a God send for both of us, but the green rolling hills of New York with their fall beauty and lonely solitude of winter sabbath will always be home to me. So many memories of hardship, strife, battle, defeat, and triumph draw me up the lonely backroads I travelled for so many years with only a vision of the future to sustain me. As a young veterinarian with a family of four, I began my practice with an old car, an old house, some meager equipment, and a strong back and willing hands, a supportive family, and a heart that didn't fail me. Many were the endless nights in bitter cold, alone, in lonely and divers places, when I put my skills on the line, and dared to do or die. There was no back up. No safety net. No corporation or government to sustain me if I failed. As I look back now and see how precarious our young family's position was in the game of life, and remember all the predators that lay in wait to see us fail, I realize that whether we succeeded or failed in business and in life, depended on how we chose to fight the battle and for a time, every day was a battle. Some days it was with fear and apprehension that I dressed and put on my work boots and headed out on the road, wondering if this cow or that herd would benefit from my intervention. And still each day came and went, and we moved ahead, inch by inch, day by day, month by month and year by year. Each day began with a prayer for help and inspiration as I headed out on the road to bear and face whatever the day brought, and ended by a prayer of thanksgiving at day's end as I headed for home. These wonderful sheltered

New York hills and valleys have been my refiner. Within their boundaries I have felt the sculptor's hands working on the rough edges of my life and teaching me by quiet example, and by success and by failure the limits of my being.

This year is my thirty-fifth year practicing a profession I am still amazed and humbled to be a part of. A client yesterday came in with her sick cat. The waiting room was full of people. At the end of my examination and treatment of her cat, she said, "I just want to tell you that if I called my doctor with the symptoms I gave about my cat, it would take days to get an appointment, but your office got me in just a few hours after I called. What time do you close?" To which I replied, "When we're done. We don't go home until the last sick animal is taken care of."

I woke up at 2:00 AM thinking of things at the clinic. I couldn't go back to sleep, so I drove up the road to check on my worries. My night man was reading a book at the front desk, keeping his watch. I fed a little chihuahua that had come in earlier in the evening with neurological signs. He wolfed the food down, which gave me hope for his recovery. I turned a fan off, turned off a bunch of lights, and turned off the air conditioning. When I was satisfied everything was battened down, I got in my truck and headed for home. It was 3:00 AM. I drove past our neighbor's house and pulled into our driveway. I saw my neighbor on his front lawn in his pajamas with his old dog struggling to walk. I had seen her a couple of days earlier and treated her. She's very old and struggling with mobility problems. I walked down the driveway to see how she was doing and how my neighbor was holding up. We visited a bit, and I made sure they were doing OK then headed back to my bed. Thirty-five years into my career still finds me excited about the ways I can help my four-legged friends and their caretakers. A mother's work is never done, and neither is a veterinarian's. I have used this body to its fullest extent. Thank you, Lord, for the road I've traveled. No regrets.

9 781493 148240